-11-90	gap plaid shorts w/ black gap turtle neck sweater,
-12-90	units midcalf pants with moms eddie bauer sweatshirt
-15-90	guess jean skirt w/ cape isle knitters sweater
-16-90	guess jeans w/ stacys forest & navey gap shirt.
-17-90	gap green shorts w/ navey & green top
-18-90	light guess jeans mom's cape isle knitters sweater
-19-90	express jeans w/ eddie bauer navy pale mint
-22-90	esprit plaid skirt w/ fo...
-23-90	gap dark jeans w/ su... gap.
-24-90	gap light jeans w/ color...
-25-90	glicks jeans w/ eddie b... yet
-26-90	gap hood sweatshirt w/ expre...
-29-90	dark guess blue jeans w/... le,
-30-90	gap jean shorts w/ stacys... shirt
-31-90	light guess jeans w/ eddie bauer polo
1-1-90	gap white jean shorts w/ gap navey & mar
-5-90	green army express jeans w/ orgiol sox
-6-90	glicks jeans w/ moms famous sweater & blue
-7-90	light guess jeans w/ forest & marron benttan sive
-8-90	dark blue gap jeans eddie bauer plaid flann
1-9-90	light gap jeans w/ j crew rugby
-12-90	dark guess jeans w/ picture sweater
-13-90	guess jean skirt w/ pasta mauve & navey sweater
-14-90	glicks jeans w/ dads red white & blue rugby
-15-90	gap jean shorts w/ moms torquoise & navey s.s.
-16-90	express jeans w/ eddie bauer grapy green marron white
-19-90	light gap jeans with eddie bauer green & peach oxford

CRINGE

C·R·I·N·G·E

Teenage Diaries, Journals, Notes, Letters, Poems,
and Abandoned Rock Operas

EDITED BY
Sarah Brown

CROWN PUBLISHERS
NEW YORK

Library of Congress Cataloging-in-Publication Data

Brown, Sarah, 1977–
Cringe: teenage diaries, journals, notes, letters, poems, and abandoned rock operas /
Sarah Brown.
p. cm.
1. Diaries—Humor. 2. Teenagers—Humor. I. Title.

PN6231.D62B76 2008
818'.602—dc22

2007045819

ISBN 978-0-307-39358-6

Printed in Singapore

Design by Elizabeth Van Itallie

1 3 5 7 9 10 8 6 4 2

First Edition

For Mom, Dad, and Stephen

Danger—
Beware

DANGER
HANDS
OFF

12/16/90
I hate every single
human 11½ year old
male that ever lived.

05 March 1994 Saturday

So the first entry of my journal is one of frustration and pain. Well, I guess its appropriate, since so much of those emotions abound in my romantic life. Everyone's I suppose. I was just wondering why such an unstable and hurtful thing can be such a dominant and encompassing aspect in ~~spect thing can be~~ aspect in ~~everyone's~~ everyone's life. Romance.. love.. "doesn't take much to rip us into pieces" (Tori Amos) Time with ___ is so scarce. He promised me we'd go out, Tonight. I s___ ___ you sure? He said yes. So all day I've ___ ___ ing I'd have fun tonight. So 1030

Its Saturday night. I'm eating brownies. Who needs love?
I've got chocolate.

have so much on my mind. I'm so depressed.
Sometimes I just give up all faith in living.
There's nothing for me! I'm so ugly and
un popular and I don't have any friends to
confide to anymore. Everybody's got their life
to live but me. I want to do it! I want
to kill myself! I want it to be over with.
I'm a failure in everything. Mom and Dad
fight all the time, and obviously no one really
likes me. I'm so ashamed of myself because
I'm so weak. Oh, make it go away! Make the
Pain stop, God... why do you punish me so bad?
I just wish I could crawl in a corner and
die.

Dear Whatever

Dear Whats-your-name

Dear Always,

Dear Diary,

Dear Diary
I h i

YAWN!!

Dear Diary,

Dec. 7, 1973

Dear Pam
I Fel

Hello World!

Dear Diary,

Dear Journal,

~~Dear Dear,~~
Dear Diary,

Dear Dad,

Dear ———

Dear Diary!
Cindy
1976 21

Sterling QUALITY

54 SHEETS — 4 IN. x 6 IN.
C-46 OPEN SIDE   MEMO BOOK   C-64 OPEN END
Mfd. by F. L. Russell Corp., Mt. Marion, N.Y. 12456

Dear Tel,

29¢

Contents

One Year Diary

Sarah Brown

Introduction

The first question everyone always asks is, Why would you do this?

I started my first diary in kindergarten. Every night, while my mother made dinner, I'd sit on the kitchen floor and write in it, asking her how to spell each word. "How do you spell today? How do you spell we? How do you spell went?" And then I'd warn her, "Do NOT read my diary." I wrote in green Strawberry Shortcake marker and ended each entry with, "I wonder what will happen tomorrow!"

FEBRUARY 23

> The Diary is Myne
> I Got it to Day This
> is February 23, 1983.
> Today We Mad Es-no Eggs
> I Wundr Waet wil happn
> Tommwy

I eventually moved on to composition notebooks and less optimistic entries. I spent the majority of my adolescence holed up in my bedroom, listening to mix tapes and doing what my friend Erin calls "journaling through some rage." By the time I was twenty-three and in my own apartment, my parents called me to come get the giant box of old notebooks still stowed under my bed.

One night I took a stack of diaries from middle school over to a friend's house and read some selections aloud while we killed a box of wine. She laughed so hard I decided it was totally worth selling out my thirteen-year-old self. This led to the Sarah Journal e-mails, where I'd send the most painful excerpts to my

friends in a weekly e-mail. This garnered a surprisingly large response, as the list grew to sixty people, forty of whom I didn't even know. Every week, right before hitting "send," I would think, "Why am I doing this again? This is embarrassing!" And then all those people would write back about how funny it was, how they remembered the same things, and suddenly the new mission was to find a more humiliating entry for the next e-mail. Which wasn't hard.

A few years later, now living in New York, I wanted to take this concept to a more public venue. The Cringe Reading Series was born at Freddy's Bar and Backroom in Brooklyn on April 6, 2005, with six brave souls reading aloud from their teenage writings to a packed house, and it's been that way ever since.

Many people ask why there seems to be such a wave of teenage reflection and recollection lately. Our society definitely likes to fetishize teenagers, and geek culture is no longer on the fringes. We who

have grown up with MTV are accustomed on some level to having our lives recorded for us and played back for our own amusement. But Cringe is more than self-absorption or nostalgia. It's natural to look back, to wonder who you were then. Surprise: pretty much who you are now, especially when things get emotional, just buried under layers of experience and better clothing choices.

I'm convinced now that the world is made up of three groups: people  who never kept diaries, people who kept diaries, and people who kept diaries but destroyed them. You have to have a sense of humor about yourself to be able to look back like this. You can't take yourself too seriously. I always tell people who are unsure what to read at Cringe to pick

the excerpt that physically makes them cringe when they read it to themselves, the one that makes you think, "I can't read that part." But then when you do, and the room erupts in laughter and everyone groans, you suddenly think, "Oh, I can top that." You are among your people. We were all the same teenager underneath. We were all sweating the same shit.

Everyone bitches about teenagers being so sensitive, which is true, but the flip side of that coin is that they're also ridiculously buoyant. "God hates me, my parents are divorcing, but I LOVE THE CURE!" When everything is the same level of urgency, you lose your sense of scale. You couldn't pay me all the money in the world to be that age again, but I do miss that intensity sometimes. The downs were awful, but the ups were pretty nice. Being a teenager is like being on drugs, only with less freedom and more dental hygiene.

Finally, it doesn't seem fair to ask everyone else to bare their own tortured teenage soul without baring mine first, so here you go.

January 5, 1991

Today was Saturday, and Jennifer and I went to the mall. We ran into Stephanie and Kristin, and we all ate lunch together. I bought the FREEDOM single by George Michael, Stephen's birthday present, Mom's birthday present, and some Sour Patch Kids when we all stopped by Moncurs. Then Jennifer and I went off on our own again. We saw Josh Rice and Brian Grigor and talked to them for awhile. Then, when we were leaning over the balcony on the upper level, we saw him — and two girls. (It struck me that one day short of a year ago, he was also with two girls, but the girls were me and Kristin and we were at a movie, not the mall.) I said, "Oh God Jennifer, do you know who that is?" Jennifer, who knows about him, nodded and said, "Let's go." Then we ran into him again, by the elevator downstairs, and this time he saw me. I pointed to a guy leaning over the balcony, and Jennifer caught on quick and said, "He's cute!" Then we laughed and walked off. The third and last time we saw each other, Jennifer and I were in Musicland, playing "Stairway to Heaven" on the keyboard and laughing. I was laughing and my hair (thank God I curled it today!) fell over my shoulder and I KNOW I looked good. Then I looked *up, and there he was, five feet away, like he was waiting to say something. I know that if he had spoken he'd have said, "Sarah?" I just smiled, kind of waved, and went on playing around. He smiled too, and I've been wondering for the past 3 months if he still has braces, and he smiled showing his teeth, and I DON'T REMEMBER. That's driving me crazy, because I'm a detail person and I SHOULD remember. Oh, well. He was wearing jeans, a purple-and-black striped rugby shirt, and a white turtleneck underneath. He looked good.*

January 5, 1991

Today was Saturday, and Jennifer and I went to the mall. We ran into Stephanie and Kirstin, and we all ate lunch together. I bought the FREEDOM single by George Michael [I still own this], Stephen's birthday present, Mom's birthday present, and some Sour Patch Kids. . . . Then, when we were leaning over the balcony on the upper level, we saw him—and two girls . . . I said, "Oh my God, Jennifer, do you know who that is?" Jennifer, who knows about him, nodded and said, "Let's go." [So here's the thing: I was in love with this guy all through middle school and high school, but could never ever bring myself to actually write his name in my diary. He is forever "Him," like Jesus.] Then we ran into him again, by the elevator downstairs, and this time he saw me. I pointed to a guy leaning over the balcony and Jennifer caught on quick and said, "He's cute!" [This is the same way I deal with men I like today. It still works just as well, by which I mean not at all.] Then we laughed and walked off. The third and last time we saw each other, Jennifer and I were in Musicland, playing "Stairway to Heaven" on the keyboard and laughing. [Note: dudes love this.] I was laughing and my hair (thank *God* I curled it today!) fell over my shoulder and for once I KNOW I looked good. [This phrase appears in my diary at an alarming number. Huge ego hiding under the guise of poor self-esteem?] Then I looked up, and there he was, five feet away, like he was waiting to say something. I know if he had said something, it would have been, "Sarah?" [Perhaps I was psychic?] I just smiled and kind of waved and went on playing around. [Good tactic, when you want desperately to talk to someone: not talking to them.] He smiled too, and I've been wondering for the past 3 months if he still has his braces, and he smiled showing his teeth, and I DON'T REMEMBER. That's driving me crazy, because I'm a detail person and I SHOULD remember. Oh, well. He was wearing jeans, a purple-and-black striped rugby shirt, and a white turtleneck underneath. He looked good.

I'm not going to call him. [I totally called him.]

May 31, 1988

B-Day List (so far):

- lion watch [received]
- new clothes
- dangle ring (silver) [Was forbidden by my mother to wear dangle rings because "what if you were climbing a ladder and it got caught on something and tore your finger off." See later in life: reasons I was not allowed to ride in Jennifer's convertible.]
- pink ghetto blaster from Service Merchandise [received]
- La Bamba tape [received]
- books—Green Sky series by Zilpha Keatley Snyder [Did not receive, but finding these diaries at twenty-six prompted me to check them out of the library. Not so good at twenty-six.]
- film for my camera
- subscription to *Teen* magazine [Was not allowed to read *Seventeen*, I guess due to its "Sex and Your Body" column? My mother would prefer I have neither.]

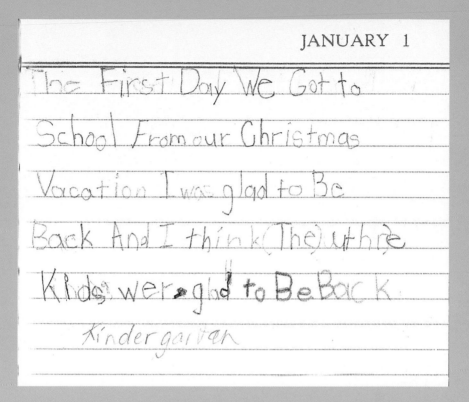

JANUARY 1

The First Day We Got to
School From our Christmas
Vacation I was glad to Be
Back And I think (The) uthre
Kidos wer glad to Be Back
kindergarten

November 25, 1988

Today Erin and I are reading each others' diaries. It's funny because in one of my diaries, I was in kindergarten and I spelled everything wrong. I bet when I wrote those kindergarten entries I never would have thought that I'd laugh when I read them in sixth grade. Someday when I'm in eleventh grade, I'll probably read THIS and laugh. But then, maybe I won't.

Sarah Brown
New York
August 2007

GLOW IN THE DARK

What is a dream —
a magical thing,
a rainbow of joy in your heart,
Your own secret corner
where no one can go,
where the path to fulfillment
can start.
A dream lures you on,
always one step ahead
until you have caught it, and then,
There's always another
to capture your soul
and lead your heart onward again.

1 Defining My Bullshit

About

Me

The best way to break in a new diary is to let it know who you are. Whether or not you tell it the truth is up to you.

Isn't it cute when six-year-olds talk about their past and refer to it as "when I was a kid"? When brand-new teenagers look back on being slightly younger teenagers and paint it as a rosy growth experience, you want to physically shield them from the inevitable train wreck of adolescence that's right around the corner. It won't all be slow dancing at homecoming dances and bonfires on the beach. You are going to cry during an assembly, you are going to puke in someone's stepdad's bathroom, and you are going to give yourself a ridiculous haircut, all because of some guy named Travis. Welcome! Enjoy! Run!

Do You Have Any Comic Books?
* Greg Howard

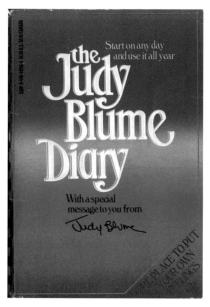

When I was in the sixth grade, my mother inexplicably gave me an official Judy Blume diary for Christmas. I think she did it because I liked *Tales of a Fourth Grade Nothing* back when I was, you know, actually in the fourth grade. I was too embarrassed to touch it for months, but eventually I wrote up the story of a schoolyard fight and also deigned to fill out the "About Me" page.

I often wondered if receiving an official Judy Blume diary meant my mother thought I was feminine. But in re-reading what I wrote, it's obvious that she had good reason for thinking so—I apparently went around saying that I liked "stuff that makes me look glamorous," like a little pint-sized Liberace. I'm also not clear why I suggested a fondness for "rock n roll parties" as I had never been invited to any, although it's likely that I had been allowed to watch *Grease* one too many times.

I still hate most of the things on my "Hate" list. Hikes can be nice.

My name is *Gregory Laweronce Howard*

Please call me *Greg* the *Great* (No relation to Sheila Tubman)

I like *Comics, girls, The Greatest American Hero, rock n roll, parties, fun, space stuff, adventures, books, and stuff that makes me look glamorous.*

I hate *School, fights, poison oak, acne, crime, snobs, Ronald Reagan, peas, hikes, manners, and people with no sense of humor!*

This year in school *will be told probably later in this package called Judy Blume's (yes, Judy Blume!) diary. Do you have any comic books?*

From *Are You There God? It's Me, Margaret.*

Some material in this diary may not be suitable for children or adults.

April 1,
April Fools
Day

Dear Diary
I have a head
ache.

████████ might have Herpes —
Natasha & Troy are
having problems —
████████ had an abortion —

I'm on my 3rd Snickers.

Problems, Descending Importance
* Kristine Smith

Freshman year of college. I was worried about my friends and, I think, my period.

I don't remember if Natasha and Troy's problems were on the abortion/herpes level, or just the third Snickers level.

That makes me think of Dante's *Inferno* with its levels of hell. Which is appropriate, because the third circle was for gluttons.

As far as Natasha and Troy, their intense problems were always sixth or seventh circle. Sigh. I was always so jealous of their relationship.

When I'm Thirty-two * Sandra Heikkinen

When I'm thirty-two [a little under two years from now, for the record], I'm fairly sure my life isn't going to be anything much like the one the eleven-year-old girl with pigtails and a lip bumper—the new black of retainers at that point, or so I was told—imagined while sitting in my sixth-grade classroom.

See, while I wrote the "composition" because I was assigned to, the assignment didn't really matter; I was enough of a mini nerd at that point that I'm pretty sure I would have anyway. A planner and half book-dork extraordinaire, I had actually visited the veterinary school at Michigan State, with green-and-white friendship pins on my Keds and a matching sweatshirt as my top, in preparation for my eventual attendance. I thought about details a lot, as is rather apparent when looking back at statements like "if my husband isn't allergic to pets . . ." and ". . . adopted or mine I'm not sure of quite yet," and I took life pretty seriously, not to mention lived rather earnestly, for an elementary-school kid.

But although I will not, in all likelihood, spend my thirty-second year living in a colonial house in Michigan, with two kids named partially after my parents, looking after four dogs—or boarding two horses and staring into the eyes of the husband I found immediately postcollege as part of my search for "the right man to marry"—I did get one thing right, and that's that anything can happen after thirty-two. Or any time, for that matter.

December 6, 1988   Sandra Heikkinen
                Composition

When I'm 32 (twenty years from now)
I hope my life will be in running order.
I want to have a colonial house, somewhat
like the one I live in now. I'll live in
Michigan when I'm 32 for no reason other
then Michigan is the best and I want
my kids to grow up in Michigan. I'll
have two kids (hopefully a boy and a
girl,) adopted or mine I'm not sure of
quite yet. If I do have a boy and a
girl I'll name the girl Laura Jean (the
Jean after my moms middle name). I
would name my boy David Douglas
(Douglas after my dad.) When I graduate
I'll go to Stanford pre-vet school,
when those years are over I'll go to
Michigan State as Stanford has no
Veterinary School. After I'm out of
college I'll go looking for the right
man to marry. If my husband isn't
allergic to pets then I'll have four dogs
    Shih Tzu a German Shorthair an Irish Setter
and a Beagle! I'll also have 2 horses and board the
    And after 32 well, anything could happen

I find myself collectively insane

I'm not an individual.
These days everyones an individual.
together.

You could see they're individuals

I sleep through
Why don't people like me?
I write slowly. and I don't do whole I have to figure out by myself?
Usually I doesn't up going at all. Sometimes I wait.
Why? who knows? of Isis.
more

If I was someone else I wouldn't be here.
If I had character. (BIG IF.) I'd be happy. still here but happy?
Can I be heard? Can I be heard through the rain?
I like this

Didn't I used to be somebody? Maybe Ask someone
who had known me then.

Maybe I'll move.

I Find Myself Collectively Insane
* Aaron McQuade

This is just such an impossibly generic collection of teenage bullshit that it literally could have been written on any day between October of 1987 and maybe August of 1996—except that the paper is textured, so this was clearly during my "if I write on nice paper, it will make my poetry that much more poetic" phase. About a month after this was when I started using a typewriter that I got from a garage sale for $5.50.

Some thoughts:
- I clearly had no idea what the word *collectively* meant.
- "People" = Erika. (See "Captain E" on page 190 for more details.)
- I'd love to tell you that my penmanship self-criticism was a metaphor for the way I tend to mishandle and neglect my relationships, but I'm pretty sure it was me being all cool with stream of consciousness. Problem is, there was nothing even remotely interesting going on in my consciousness.
- The worst part about going through a shoebox is remembering being proud of crap like this. Even worse is not being able to pretend that I *wasn't* proud of it.

Didn't I used to be somebody? Maybe. Ask someone
Who had known me then.   Maybe I'll move.

I want
identity

- At the end of sixth grade I was voted "most musical" for my drumming skills, as well as "class clown" and "best personality." But by ninth grade I was nothing more than a washed-up has-been whose glory days had passed me by. Oh, how I longed for my youth.

31

Editor's Note:

"Who wrote this?"

"President Tollini. You know, that outgoing woman who cured cancer."

Aug. 18, 1989 (Friday)

I went to the mall with Deana today + I finished up my school shopping. Woo,000! I really need is ribbon + a watch. Picked up my (smiley) shirt + jeans yesterday, fine jeans go →

It's so strange - in 9 months I'll be a teenager, so if you go from baby to kid to teenager to adult what are we supposed to accomplish while we're a kid? What are you ever?

(cont.) CHART!!!

The questions are crazy - The answers are free!

Question #1. Could buy one tape - who two would it be? Hangin' Tough/ - New kids on the Block

2. Fave song? (I'm) walkin' on Sunshine! - Katrina + the Waves

3. Could meet anyone, who would it be? #1 birth George on @ N.K.O.T.B.

(3.) Many Bon Fetish?

4. One wish? Another sister!

5. In 10 years what or who do you think you'd be in 10 years? 20 year olds... I'd be married with a kid & I'll probable -

I, Justice a mother, that's like to skate, dance, etc!!! - HA!

wants to be like that - Even - I'm not like that now! I want to be known as fun, smart & caring with a sense of humor. It's like by the time you're 8 people have you figured out... when I was a kid people thought I was stupid in math - still am!, stupid funny. Now I'm out going, smart + funny. But people will always think of me as the dumb kid with the fluffy hair who dressed like a geek.

supposed to accomplish? Caused by the times! I find out who I am of what I want to do it'll be too late. I see all these teenagers + they all seem the same - they have boyfriends/ hang out at malls all day, flunk tests, + play Metallica tapes on head phones. They dress in whatever hats, & aaa they care about is how they look + what to wear. I don't

"You mean that dumb kid with the fluffy hair who dressed like a geek?"

Writing words to songs always helps me calm down. that last one I wrote I think reminds me of Dan Z. in a way. I mean, I guess if I had stayed with him I'd never realize what real love is because what we had wasn't really real. He was cheating on me from day 1. I just hope I don't get stuck in that kind of relationship ever again. I guess that's what I'm scared of. I'm scared of misjudging someone else and getting myself hurt again. Boy - this is the last page of yet another journal. Cool - I get to move on to another one. I wonder if someday these things will be worth anything? Who knows? Maybe my kids (Hi Hope!) will like them. I wonder if I'll marry someone I know now. I doubt it. I'm sure I'll have a million more boyfriends before I find the right one. The right one - gosh sometimes I wonder if there's really such a thing. I hope so. I hope I find someone to fall hopelessly in love with some day. I guess until then I'll have fun with all these wrong ones. Well - no more room. Adios and Gd. Bless you. Love - Erinn

Worth Anything * Erinn Foley

It's frightening, really: the words I was writing when I was fifteen years old are very close to the way I often feel today. If you had told me when I was that young, that by the year I turned thirty I'd still be playing with all the "Mr. Wrongs" of the world, I would have considered you an absolute moron. I was certainly right about "a million more boyfriends," that's for sure. And yes, I certainly still wonder if there is such a thing as "the right one."

"I wonder if someday these things will be worth anything?"

Probably not. Maybe $22.95, tops.

Throw your day-planner out the window— you're a fly-by-the-seat-of-your-designer-pants chick. A total chameleon, even your closest friends can't predict what you're going to do next.

libra

(Sep. 23–Oct. 22)

Your look: All-out glam.
Your beauty personality: Sexy styles psych you up, and you can pull them off while still managing to look sweet and innocent.
Standout feature: Your delicate nose.
Beauty treat: An aromatherapy candle to calm you.
Best color: Scarlet
Best hairstyle: A messy updo—you were born for it!
Worst beauty habit: Wearing way too much perfume. Try an eau de toilette instead so you pack less of a fragrance punch.
Perfect product: A pretty compact, like the Forever Compact from Clinique, for public touch-ups.
Dare to try: Adding rhinestone clips to your 'do.
Guys love your look because: It says, "I'm a flirting goddess!"

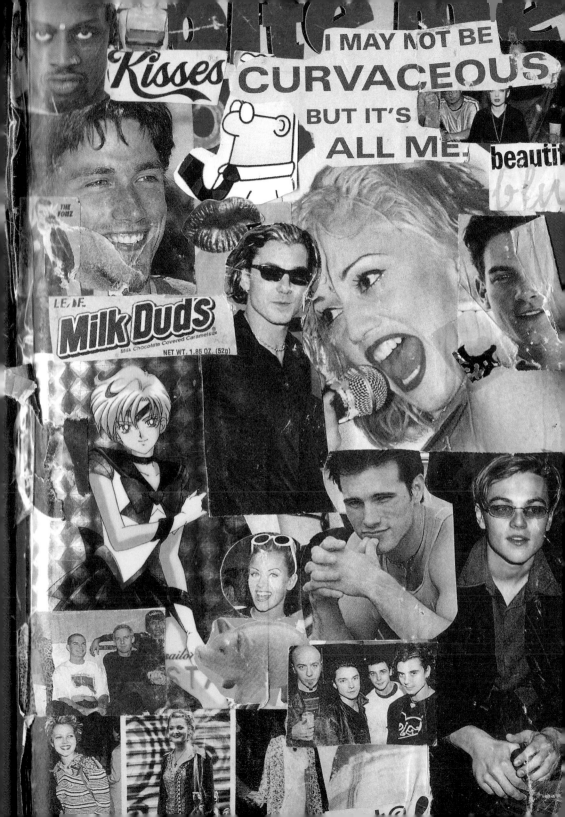

One day I shall just snap and explode and go mad and murder many people. No, I wont. But its a nice thought.

I am feeling insecure and inadequate now since I saw all of those people. I am so boring and plain and average and mediocre and uninteresting and not unique at all. I look so boring. I am normal looking. It's scary. I want to do something truly unique to my apearance.

I think I looked pretty nice, but I geuss not, because no one, not even the usual nerds asked me to dance.

BLUE

Tues.
July 27, 1982

Dear Diary,

YAWN!!

EASYTEAR
Bobby Brown

...ast n... sm...
the first... n m...
...ell n... lly...
it. I s... a smo...
ge... in my ...un...
ac...nt and...
except make me co...
It was fun wh...
It tasted like old stale coffee and rotten cold peppermint and buttercream. Quite a combination. I liked blowing it out of my mouth. Smoking is a disgusting habit that I will probably do again unfortunately. I also drank some beer. I dont know why but I did. It was very fuzzy and didnt taste as bad as it usually does. I did not get drunk.

!!!!I am being corrupted!!!!

2 Being a Better Horrible You

Self-H

elp

There's nothing more excruciating or heartbreaking than the self-help lists teenagers make for themselves. You know you're a mess, you know you need help, and you know absolutely nothing about anything. It's like trying to write a trig textbook before you've learned long division. But don't let that stop you. Improvement all boils down to patience, confidence, perseverance, and not gagging.

Most of these lists smack of every single issue of *Seventeen*. And probably *Cosmo* and *Glamour* and *Field & Stream*. Pretty much every magazine in existence could run these exact steps with very little editing.

Take Calcium Pills * Margaret Mason

This is an incredibly anal list of New Year's Resolutions from when I was eleven. It's chilling to realize that you've been working on pretty much the same shit since you were in sixth grade.

I was a tightly wound eleven-year-old, and apparently I'm a tightly wound thirty-one-year old. Geez. Re-reading these resolutions made me realize that my essential nature will never be thwarted. You're either a regular flosser or you ain't. Don't fight the flow.

Date **Continued**

New Years Resolutions

1. Keep my room clean.
2. Start writing down appointments,
3. Give mom school notes.
4. Write more letters.
5. Be more responsible,
6. Brush my teeth.
7. Save money.
8. Take calcium pills.
9. Start X-mas shopping early.
10. Eat less sugar,
11. Eat square meals.
12. Jog or cycle,
13. Exercise more.
14. Turn off lights.
15. Iron your own clothes
16. Do more socially,
17. Finish what you start

Rosewater's tips on giving a nice blow job

Posted to a BBS, fall 1992

Number 1: Take your time.

Number 2: Imitate your mouth to be almost like a vagina. (Here, I apologize for the fact that I was raised by a nurse/midwife and I always use medical terms. Sorry.) Your lips should always be wet. Lick them if you need to.

Number 3: Stroke the length of the penis with your tongue in the hardened KISS (rock group) extended way.

Number 4: Listen carefully to hear what he is feeling and enjoying the most. And even tease him a bit.

Number 5: When it is evident that the male in question is about to cum, take a deep breath and stick as much of his penis as possible in your mouth. DO NOT PUT IT IN SO FAR AS TO GAG!! This is not enjoyable for either one of you! Gagging on a penis is a hell, and hearing a girl gag is a real turn-off. So, avoid that. But it does feel good to the guy, and then when he comes it will go straight down your throat instead of swishing around in your mouth. Mmm: yum. Nothing better than that warm, salted, melted-milkshake-with-extra-iron-supplements taste. PUKE!

Um, that's all. Remember that I wrote this from my own experience (which is not all that extensive - only one guy) and for myself, so it may not pertain to you at all.

Rosewater's BJ Tips * Ariel Meadow Stallings

Despite being a geeky drama queen, in 1992 I finally scored myself a boyfriend because, hell, even weird geeky girls have boobs, and for some seventeen-year-old boys, that's all that really matters. And as a nerdy know-it-all, I couldn't simply let my sexual awakening slip by . . . I had to share my newly developed knowledge and expertise with people by writing these naïve blow job tips on a BBS, which was an early '90s version of a Web message board.

One of the big advantages of being an early adopter geek is that you get to say you embarrassed yourself on the Internet before most people had even heard of e-mail.

Serenity
Betrayal
Laziness
Selfishness

1. Suspense is waiting to see if you get to go to Putt-Putt.
2. Suspense is waiting to see if you won a video game tournament or not.
3. Suspense is waiting to see what you got on your test.

1. Gluttony is when you go to McDonald's and order three hamburgers with everything on it and a large coke, two ice cream cones, and a large french fries.
2. Gluttony is eating three pieces of pizza, a box of cookies, three bags of b-b-q potato chips and a two ice cream sudaes for hot lunch.

1. Serenity is watching Three's Company every minute of every day.
2. Serenity is not having school.
3. Serenity is watching anything you want anytime you want.

1. Betrayal is when your best friend catches a fly ball and he has your mitt.
2. Betrayal is when your favorite teacher cuts you off the baseball team.

1. Laziness is when you know an answer in class but you are too tired to raise your hand.
2. Laziness is when you dive for a baseball and you miss but you are too tired to go get it.

46

Enthusiasm
Modesty
Embarassed

Sneakiness
Contentment
Tension
Exaggeration

(3) Laziness is when your favorite movie is on and you fall asleep.

(4) Selfishness is when you mark all the labels on the food in your cupboard so nobody can eat them.

(2) Selfishness is when you hide all of the sweets and your mom was sure she bought some.

(1) Generosity is giving someone all of your quarters at the arcade.

(2) Generosity is letting someone have your piece of candy on your birthday.

(1) Modesty is getting an A on a test and saying it was nothing.

(2) Modesty is getting on a television program and saying I'm not that good of an actor.

(3) Modesty is getting 266,400 on Donkey Kong and telling everyone it was a bad score.

(1) Sneakiness is staying home from school on the day of an exam when you're not sick.

(2) Sneakiness is eating in class when the teacher said not to eat, a second before.

(1) Contentment is going to an arcade every day.

(2) Contentment is having your own video games.

(3) Contentment is not having homework.

(1) Tension is waiting to see if your on the baseball team or not.

Quick, Finish *To the Lighthouse* Before Your Nails Dry * Gabrielle Fine

I wrote this when I was seventeen, and going through my Goddess/girl power phase. This was an attempt to rise up above the lovelorn pangs of teenage unrequited infatuation; my crush was away at college and the fate of our shaky relationship uncertain. When not busy pining away (and somewhat enjoying the drama of doing so), I would take long baths and listen to Tori Amos to affirm to myself that I was a BEAUTIFUL GODDESS who didn't NEED ANY MAN.

Fifteen years later, I am both embarrassed and charmed by my naïve, fragile seventeen-year-old attempts to bolster what was a wavery self-esteem at best. I must have been unaware of the irony; as I mull over my bubbly, optimistic script I can't help but wonder if I was completely in earnest or if there was any dollop of sarcasm. I had, after all, already adopted a mostly black wardrobe at that point, although I never could adopt the requisite world weariness to match and remained disgustingly bright-eyed.

Uh . . . GIRL POWER!

Being a Goddess

a. Take a hot bath. Find some bath salts or bubbles that make you feel absolutely divine: AROMATHERAPY. Find a candle & call it your "goddess candle", used specially for this occasion.

b. Watch yourself in the mirror. You are so cute.

c. Play a tape that you made specially for yourself - not Him - w/ such songs as Voice Of the Beehive, Sinéad O'Connor, Neneh Cherry, Annie Lennox, Tori Amos.

d. Wear whatever you want.

e. Put on a face mask or Noxzema and walk around the house singing. Sketch a portrait of yourself. You are so cute.

f. Give yourself a complete pedicure, & manicure too. Massage your feet. They are so cute.

g. Dance.

h. Read books by such people as Alice Walker, Virginia Woolf, Kate Chopin's The Awakening, Betty Friedan's Feminine Mystique, Isabel Allende

i. Write your own personal version of the Declaration of Independence. Write a poem (about how cute you are.) Do something you've never done before.

j. Call your closest female friend and totally diss every guy in the universe.

People to stay away from for
a while / how to identify:

I

A. HOODS
  1. Boys with hair past their shoulders
  2. Girls with hair layered a lot or
spiked or bangs 6" taller than their scalp
  3. Either boys or girls dressed
All in black or wearing Metallica, etc.
paraphenalia
  4. Anyone who smells strongly of smoke.
  5. People who've flunked more than 2-3 times
B. ODDBALLS
  1. Kids who think knock-knock,
elephant, or other dumb jokes are funny
  2. ANYONE wearing two different kinds of
socks, or only one sock
  3. Boys who's underwear are sticking
out of the back of their jeans
  4 Girls who like boys who's underwear
stick up out of their jeans
  5. kids who pick their noses and
wipe it under their desks

People to Stay Away from for a While / How to Identify * Sarah Niersbach

Knock, knock: who's there? A friendless, bitchy eleven-year-old! Why I had no friends was a mystery that tortured me at the time . . . I was more into making lists at the time than into figuring it out, I guess. What's funny is, a lot of the people I hang out with now are the ones whom I was trying to avoid back then; the kids who wore "Metallica, etc. paraphenalia" in middle school.

Who this list was meant for, I have no idea. I know I personally did wear two different colored socks on multiple occasions in a sorry attempt to look cool, and I would have sold my soul for the ability to tease my hair up more than six inches. And let's be honest: I totally picked my nose and wiped it under my desk more than once. However, that last bit is pretty sound advice. No good ever came from a girl who liked a boy whose underwear stuck up out of his jeans.

Warren: THE PLAN * Erinn Foley

This makes me cringe to this day . . . the efforts that my friend Brooke and I went to in order to attempt to secure boyfriends. And they never did seem to work! For all the nights we spent as cohorts to these elaborate schemes, what really came of that time? At least I kept a solid friendship from it all, because the boys sure are long gone.

At fourteen, the most convoluted plans seemed totally simple and entirely plausible. How would you get his attention? Say hello? Hell no. That would be so embarrassing.

November 27, 1994

<u>THE PLAN</u>

Talk to him about twice a week - inconspicuous

if I call & he doesn't call back - it counts

Brooke goes to meet Warren's friends, and I, of
course, have to go ~~with~~ also. Spend time - 4 of us.
Hopefully Brooke hits it off - fakes if not. Good
time - happy relys off. Warren thinks - friend
spend night. Friend talks of Brooke - which
makes Warren think of Erin. Warren tells
Daniel, reluctantly, that he likes Erin.
Waits for Daniel's reaction. If good
Warren says "Go for it." If medium Warren
goes for it slowly. If bad, ~~keeps~~ we
reevaluate situation.

STEP 1 - <u>Have confidence</u>! Keep your head up, smile, and be aware! Watch out for embarrassing situations! They are what you need least now! I can avoid these by watching myself. No more tripping down the bleachers in Brian ████████ face. That is

(P.3)→ definately the wrong way to go for a kiss! No matter what happens my head will be up & I'll be smiling my secure smile. I won't let anyone or thing get me down!!!

STEP 2 - <u>Conquer Ground</u>. If I'm friends w the person (this at least goes for Randy) stake things out at the beginning. Make sure the guy is <u>not</u> going out w anyone! If he just likes someone it doesn't matter, I can change that. If someone is goin' out with someone, forget them. Don't get involved I said I won't let anyone get me down. Well if I find out too late that someone's taken, that plan could be blown. So watch out!

STEP 3 - <u>Turn on the charm</u>! Be as fucking nice as you can be. Guys go crazy over compliments. As long as they're true, say 'em. Guys know if they're true, & if they are they feel awesome that you know it! They'll have a new respect for you knowing that. This can't really be considered kissing up, because it's actually manipulation. The guys don't know it, but you are actually getting into his mind to do what you want it to!

STEP 4 - <u>Eye contact</u> - you have gorgeous eyes Lori, you know it, everyone tells you so, so go ahead and use them. You can make them twinkle, or look confused, or cute, or innocent or anything. You use them to get anything you want. Use it for this. In the halls link eyes will <u>all</u> guys & give the impression you want. To make a lasting impression, give the guy a long, slow, eye-connecting stare, then slowly look away. The guy'll be so busy wondering eyes

STEP 5 - <u>Smile, smile, smile</u>!!! When ya aren't giving "the eyes", smiles work like charms! Smile about everything. It shows confidence - a quality that everyone likes in someone. Don't let anyone get you down - laugh over it - people will admire you! And in the halls link eyes <u>and</u> smile - it kills the guys - they feel so loved. But be careful not to smile & laugh too much, people will call you a ditz or think your the village idiot.

STEP 6 - <u>ESP</u> - Don't even ask how it works. I don't know, but it's worked before, and I'll try it again now! I don't know exactly how, but if you sit there while talking to a guy (or just looking at him) think hard to yourself - ya, I know you like me, stop playing games, you want me - about the guy. Somehow, your message (verbal) or look will project that message into his brain, either that or really ESP!

Steps 1–6, Memo to Myself * Lori Dalton

Will someone please tell the voices in my head that they are embarrassing me?

This was written when I was fourteen, during the winter of my freshman year of high school. Despite the metaphorical imagery of my "Memos" on either side of a fractured heart, I wasn't suffering from a broken heart at the time, or, from the sound of things ("You have gorgeous eyes, Lori"), a lack of confidence; just, apparently, too much time on my hands. Also, maybe, multiple personalities.

In any case, my "Six Steps" worked—I got a boyfriend a month later.

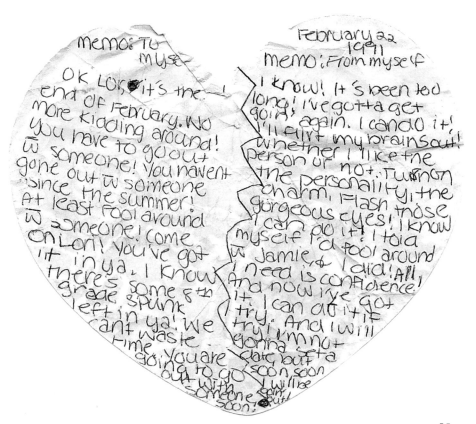

2-21-91	gap jean shorts w/ gap jean strip oxford
2-22-91	gap polka dot pants w/ navey shirt
2-25-91	gap light jeans w/ J.Crew rugby
2-26-91	guess jeans w/ mom's sweater maroon w/ white tring
2-27-91	black jeans w/ stacis N zcal sweatshirt
2-28-91	Brandis jeans w/ Gap navey green strip
3-1-91	express jean shorts w/ J.Crew navey yellow strip
3-4-91	dark gap jeans w/ army green tin gay
3-5-91	guess fring jean w/ stacy blue & green gap shi.
3-6-91	black guess jeans w/ brown black strip gap
3-7-91	light guess jeans w/ Maroon J.Crew
3-8-91	Brandis jeans w/ ~~CB SWEAT SHIRT~~
3-11-91	jean gap shorts w/ russel electric blue t-shirt
3-12-91	jean skirt w/ cape isle knitter sweater
3-13-91	light light gap jeans Miami sweatshirt
3-14-91	limited jeans w/ Michigan sweatshirt
3-15-91	polo turtel neck w/ Brandis jeans
3-18-91	Brandis jeans w/ orgial socks & sweater
3-19-91	gap light light jeans w/ navey oxtora
3-20-91	black gues jeans w/ Gap gray hood
3-21-91	guess gap jean shorts, American eagle s.s.
4-1-91	guess jean shorts w/ polo rugby
4-2-91	corona aa beer shirt w/ kake shorts
4-3-91	esprit flower shirt navey tin.
4-4-91	white shorts w/ gray hooded shirt
4-5-91	gap jean shorts w/ greatful dead t-shirt

White Gap Jean Shorts * Amy Shapiro

I never wanted to wear the exact same outfit the exact same way more than once, so I wrote down everything I wore to school every day, all throughout high school.

This entry and those found in the endpapers is from my sophomore year at Parkway North Senior High in St. Louis, Missouri. Even though my fashion was hypermanaged in my journals, I was by no means the best dressed of any given year. This was a time when fold-down button-fly jean shorts were all the rage, Express was known as Limited Express, and it was apparently OK to wear Christmas sweaters (in October). It's not really like that much has changed eighteen years later. Sure, I now know that *strip* is spelled *stripe* and that *navey* is spelled *navy*, but I still wear both stripes (strips) and navy (navey). The main difference is that the Esprit, Gap, Eddie Bauer, and Guess of my then have been replaced by the Target, H&M, Old Navy, Century 21, and Filene's Basement of my now. I no longer have a Christmas sweater, nor do I keep track of my outfits in the back of a journal, but I do try to mix it up just the same.

Just for old time's sake, today I am wearing SALT jeans from Filene's Basement with a Target wifebeater and an Old Navy cream-and-brown cardigan. I will not wear this outfit next week or the following week, believe that.

White Gap Jean Shorts, cont.

☆ ♡ (WAR) ☮ Ⓐ

4-8-91	black polo (Gap) w/ black and brown # shorts
4-9-91	white gap shorts w/ gap big strip oxford
4-10-91	emily's levi's w/ eddie Bauer sweater navey
4-11-91	gap dot paints w/ white sweatshit
4-12-91	Brandi's jeans w/ eddie Bauer granny maroon teal
7-15-91	express jeans shorts maroon J crew jersey
4-16-91	guess jean shorts w/ polo t.n. yellow
4-17-91	white gap shorts w/ gap navey maroon t.n.
4-18-91	green (army) gap t.n. Brown gap shorts
4-19-91	gap jean shorts with blue purple teal white t.n.
4-22-91	Brandi's jeans w/ gap blue & navey
4-23-91	express jean shorts w/ miami sweatshirt
4-24-91	mave navey polo eddie Bauer light light Gap jeans
4-25-91	umlted plaid shorts w/ navey gap short slevs
4-26-91	guess jean skirt w/ Jet sweater
4-28-91	Ada's shorts w/ black turtleneck
4-30-91	guess jean shorts w/ stacys gap navey green
5-1-91	gap jean shorts cream V neck sweater
5-2-91	white gap shorts w/ Blue T shirt
5-3-91	express jean shorts w/ wisconsin s.s.
5-6-91	light gap pants w/ baha
5-7-91	gap reg jeans w/ stacys navey & forest T-shirt
5-8-91	Ken's jean shorts w/ red Gap t.n.
5-9-91	Esprit flowered shorts w/ gap navey
5-10-91	Ken's jean shorts w/ gap navey & yellow
5-13-91	gap jean short w/ navey recycled angry hnksm
5-14-91	glicks cut jeans (brna gq bob shirt

5-15-91	guess jean skirts w/ stacy navey oxford snowflake
5-16-91	guess jean shorts w/ stacy's green gap w/ blue strip
5-17-91	guss light jean shorts w/ mom dark pink polo
5-20-91	gap jean shorts w/ Jo's pink v-neck sweater
5-21-91	reg. gap jeans w/ navey gap shirt
5-22-91	guess light jean shorts w/ ort sweater
5-23-91	express jean shorts w/ stacy's gap ≡ white navey gap
5-24-91	white gap gap jeans jean shorts w/ stacy's Mi Casa
5-28-91	polo turtleneck guess light jean shorts
5-29-91	gap navy shirt w/ express bandan shorts
5-30-91	guess jean skirt w/ electric blue omni shirt

3 You Ruined the Whole Family

Paren

ts

It's funny, because with some distance and years and wisdom, you can sympathize with your parents for having to live under the same roof as teenage you, even laugh about it with them. Oh, remember how I broke the bathroom door! Wasn't I awful! But then they can make one joke too many and suddenly you can tap right back into that adolescent rage at the drop of a hat. You're a grown-up now, though, so you stifle it and excuse yourself to smoke while you stand on their porch, seething, thinking, "When I get home, I'll just write in my journal about this."

SAME AS IT EVER WAS.

Probably not that much.
Whatever I totally
have a math test tomorrow
and I'm so close to being
grounded. Its not even
funny. My mom is a
total PSYCHOTIC
Seriously all she cares about
is grades, its not like
she cares about us at ALL.
Yesterday she threatened to
take away my boombox
AND my synthesizer. Doesn't
she know how important

they are to me?? I
HATE her!!!

BYE!

I HATE Her!!! BYE! · Sarah Kelly

I feel there is nothing worse in the world than being barred from your boom box and your synthesizer by a known psychotic who feels you have nothing more to offer the world than good grades, which is clearly not even something you have to offer the world.

What did I have to offer the world at the age of thirteen?

With lyrics like "sea/sea/sea of despair" and guitar riffs played on a keyboard, I was well on my way to sit by Riki Rachtman's side on MTV's *Headbangers Ball*. Everyone knew that. Had my mom not taken away the Casio CT-360 and my boom box that week before my final exams, I would be playing keys in a metal band to this day—riding high on the crest of the wave of success, doped up in a tiny Hollywood bungalow reminiscing with aging metalheads about our fallen comrades who ODed—instead of living in Brooklyn with enough sobriety to hold down a job and complete a master's program.

Dear Dad · John Sellers

My eighth-grade English teacher, a blond Dutchman with a porn-star mustache, sadistically required us to keep a writing journal. Most of my entries were short essays defending my various passions or denouncing stuff I thought sucked in 1983. But this one stands out not only because it ventures into creative writing, but also because of its obnoxious, self-congratulatory finish, which I now realize drowns in an incestuous sexual quagmire. ("I've seen him play on you, too"? Yikes.) The game described in the first paragraph, by the way, is Donkey Kong Jr. J.A.S.—that is, yours truly—loved that game.

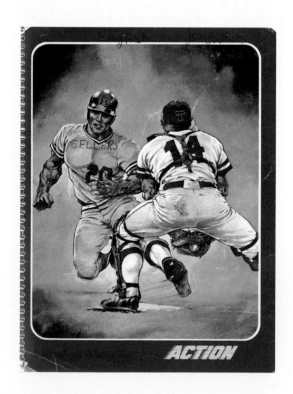

Dear Dad,

I like being a video game. How come you won't let me be one? Is it because I'm to young to be running to save you. Well, you can't stop me. I will kill the man who caged you and then you will be proud of me. Why don't you like my game, you were even in it. I hope I can kill the man who caged you before he caged me.

My best friend is across the aisle from me, Deco Bump'n' Jump. Who is your best friend? I bet it's Amidar Tracer or Yack's son. Do you like working in Putt Putt? I sure do. I like eating quarters and getting paid. Last month, I was one of the high score games. It is a little contest. When was the last time you were in the contest?

There is this one kid who plays on me who is really good. His high score is 125,000, His initials are J. A. S. I've seen him play on you, too. Words around that he's the best video game player in the whole city. He just won $20.00 in a tournament. He is great.

Sincerely Yours,
Your son.

Dear Whats-your-name

Did God make it so
that adolesnt years were
so confusing. Does he
have a grudge on me
or something? Lately mom
and dad have been
fighting A LOT!! I think
they even might get a
divorce! Oh well, it's a
part of life. Kelly's
parents are divorced and
she turned out okay.
Dad has been getting on
my case lately as well.
Every fight that happens
he blames on me. Every
mess in the house he
blames on me and
makes me clean it up.
I also have my suspsions
that he is having an affair.
It takes him 20 to 45 mins
to get a newspaper then
he says something like
"I had to go to 7 different
stores to get it" like gimme

Don't Worry, Be Happy · Hollie Pocsai

Nineteen ninety-six was a bad year for me. While I thought that I was doing all the things a normal thirteen-year-old girl should be doing—joining the Three Stooges fan club at school, watching *Captain Planet,* and reading *Tiger Beat*—my mom took these all to be warning signs that I was going to become a pregnant teenage runaway junkie. To prevent this from happening, she took it upon herself to read my diary to look for clues. And although there was no evidence of heroin or sex or Hell's Angels, there was this entry. If you think that compiling your old diary entries for a book is embarrassing, try having your parents sit you down at thirteen years old and read your diary aloud to you. Then try listening to them explain to you that your father would never cheat on your mother, that they love you very much, and sweetie, twenty to forty-five minutes isn't even long enough for your father to have an affair, but you wouldn't understand why just yet.

My parents ended up getting a divorce in the end. And actually, I don't think Kelly did turn out OK in the long run.

a break me and mom 8
aren't that stupid. Jo is
so so weird I can't
stand it! I have to go
so Bye for now!

Love,

Hollie

Pocsai

Don't worry,
Be happy

19

Dear ———   July 16 96
                9:29 pm

I am living in a
dream world. Wishes
are nothing but a
bunch of crap. They
never come true so
whats the use of
even wasting your time
trying to and hoping
they'll come true
when they don't? Shannon
told Liza a bunch of
fuckin lies and now
Liza's mad at me
for a fucking god
damn lie. Saw the
Sailor Moon movie
today. It was awsome
except there were
subtitles. My mom
thinks Sailor Moon
is like a cult I'm
like "Yah mom that's
it"

sorry felt like doing that she goes "Well what's the appeal of Sailor Moon" and I go "well what was the appeal of " the Brady Bunch and The Partridge Family?" and ⌣ ⌣ ⌣ Uhhhgg I kinda like Eric Fallon now but I'm not telling anyone not even Iris! Because like Mel and Rel are like super good friends with him. Well gotta go

LUV
n
stuff

UUUhhngg! · Hollie Pocsai

Do you know what earth-shattering event happened to make me so despondent? It was that I was forbidden to watch *Sailor Moon* from then on out, because my mom really did think it was a cult.

UUUhhngg!

Sorry. I still get enraged when I think about that. Like, it was a bunch of fucking goddamn lies.

There really is no better response to your mother at this age than "UUUhhngg!" It's all encompassing.

Mom in Love · Lori Dalton

My parents got divorced when I was five years old, and I grew up watching my mom date, hoping, for both our sakes, that she would fall in love again. In this entry, I was a fifteen-year-old sophomore, and she had just met the man who would eventually become her second husband. While I was clearly happy for her, I was also happy for what I thought it would bring me in the form of clothes, vacations, and maybe a car. To say I was self-absorbed is an understatement.

My mom is madly in love w her boyfriend ███ They've only been dating a few months, but he's moving in this month & they're gonna get married sometime. Cool! He's so rich, He has awesome clothes — and a lot! I could get a lot out of this — vacations, a car — if he buys my mom one + she gives me hers — psyche! He's 27 — another young 'un. So everyone's happy, I'm just waiting for Pete to call me back. Its 10:30pm I'm gonna go, Sayunara!

Pete

Sunday
Date Jan 12, 1992

I hate my sister. She ruined the whole family. She is so spoiled. Why can't they discipline her. I try to help + I always get hollared at towards the end. Now I have lead poisoning in my hand + every one hates me!

I'm alright now because I've written it down. I'm going to jump on tramp now.

Today we are going shopping for a dress, I hope we find one. we better

We didn't find a dress. I can't believe they didn't fit. I say I'm not going to eat a lot but I get home + pig out. I just ate a box of moms * I owe my mom $2.00.

I Have Lead Poisoning in My Hand and Everyone Hates Me · Dana A. Gulino

This is a rare glimpse into my teen life, exposing the angst and torture that a fifteen-year-old young woman endured as she struggled through her middle-class, suburban life in New Jersey, uncertain if she would make it through to another day. Sibling rivalry! Lead poisoning! Trampoline jumping! Dress shopping! M&Ms! The horror! How I made it out alive and lived to tell about it is certain to one day become an epic feature-length film that will undoubtedly score Natalie Portman an Oscar.

My younger sister was a child model. Once she hit second grade, the modeling stopped. However, the Naomi Campbell–like attitude did not. As you can see in the bottom picture, I had hair issues (among several others). Therefore, my sister's superiority complex combined with my fashion and beauty challenges created some serious jealousy on my part.

The lead in my hand? The near-fatal accident that no one in my family seemed to acknowledge in its severity? Yeah, I fell down the stairs and my hand landed on a pencil at the bottom. Lead side up. It belonged to my sister, so obviously she had planted it for me to land on, thereby almost securing my sad and tragic death by a No. 2.

Anyway, I had to shop for a dress for winter formal, and, when I didn't find one, I did what every insecure teenager across the country did: I stole the candy that my brother was selling for some fund-raiser and ate the goods in my bedroom. Then I stared at myself in the mirror and wept, perfecting my cry-face.

The Post-it Notes · Jay Carlson

I used to leave notes for my parents on the kitchen counter to let them know of my whereabouts. This sounds like a very commonsense thing to do.

However, I took the idea at more than face value and felt the medium was a great opportunity to show off the razor-sharp wit of a ninth-grader. Anyone with the gift of hindsight (and regular sight) would agree: these notes are particularly awful for myriad reasons. For one, I was fifteen years old and I had the penmanship of a gifted third-grader. And then there's that whole thing with the content of the notes being neither clever nor funny.

I don't know why my parents didn't burn these notes. I guess they saved them for sentimental reasons. Or maybe this is their way of getting me back for that time I melted the vacuum cleaner after sucking an open flame from the fireplace. Whatever the reason, I've grown to accept the mistakes from my past. Whiskey will dull my pain soon enough.

I went on my bike 'round to roam,
Before dark is when I'll be home,
The dishes away, The dog I can't say,
The mail is inside, My hey by my side.
I'm at Carrie's, Mom or Larry.
I'm sure to have fun!
From your poetic son!

                Jay.

Ode to a kid who went bike-riding,
walked the dog, put the dishes away in
the dishwasher, got the mail, went over
to Carrie's House (654-███) and will be back
by dark because he, for once, has no
homework.
           By Jay Carlson
Sorry, there's not enough room for my
poem, maybe you'll hear it another day

The Story of my life in a day
        By Jay Carlson
Chapter 1 - Writes a clever note to mom
Chapter 2 - Patch goes to the bathroom
Chapter 3 - Change of clothes; gets hey;
         empties dishwasher; bring in
        mail
Chapter 4 - Goes to Carrie's (654-███

               over

Chapter 5 - Comes home at or before dark
Chapter 6 - takes shower

If you would like to know more, Please check
out The Story of my life in a day. It's soon
to be out in a theater near you!

Test
                    Name ———
                    Date ———
                    period ———

1) Jay is
  a) riding his bike
  b) doing his homework (yeah right)

2) J a) walked the dog
  b) brought in mail
  c) a+b

                    over

---

4) Jay is Carrying...
  a) his hey
  b) hockey ruck
  c) silverware

5) $\sqrt{a^2+b^2} + \pm\sqrt{5} \ \pi \ [.2]$
  a) I give up
  b) No one knows
  c) No one Cares

                  Jay

I still think
TG + I think
KB is cute!
My parents are
the meanest
shittiest parents
in the U.S. of
A! they get on
my case every
damn day!
I wish I could
take a
vacation!!

Tuesday, September 5, 1989

today was my first day

1/26/90
at Christines
party we played
spin the bottle
I kissed Michael
L. White 3 times
and Brian Lesser
once. The party!!!
was

I am SEXUALLY
FRUSTRATED?
♡ all boys!
almost every guy I see (it seem

08 october 1
it seems
one of those
have fine
ible, outco
and you
upswing, a
in protection against the brutal
world. our love is steady an
sue, perhaps the only thing
that endures. Eli

4

I Am Having Some Feelings

Melod

rama

The thing about being a teenager is that every single thing that happens to you is huge, whether it's a fight with your parents or being heartbroken or not having the right kind of shoes; it's all RIGHT HERE, on the surface, ready to blow at all times. And when everything is the same level of importance, you lose a little bit of perspective. Which is also the awesome part of being a teenager; you can't be held accountable for jack.

Life Is Crumbling * Kitty Joe Sainte-Marie

65

24 september 1996 tuesday 130pm

life is crumbling. it has never been as empty, as worthless, as painful as this. i have never before had this much to lose, been shown the path i so desire and then been denied. i have never so rationaly contemplated ending it because it has never been so near an end. i feel like killing my physical body would only stop a whole lifetime of hollow monotony; the spiritually gutted life ahead of me. i am empty, and i stand here with nothing to fill me up.

i cannot write specifically, it is too much of a horror. i cannot see it, speak it's truth, for the one disgusting string of hope keeps me alive, refusing to be cut. i cannot speak it.

———

5pm

jesus christ! i just walked into cafe lalo and got a job! i just made something out of nothing this piece of my life has nothing to do with eli. he didn't take me there. he didn't tell me to go there. he didn't tell me how to ~~get the~~ use the fucking phone to call there. i just put ani de franco on the stereo, a particularly

If the only escape from your relationship is a job as a barista and seeking solace in Ani Difranco . . . actually, I don't know if that even qualifies as an escape.

The best part is that I have no idea what I was so upset about.

83

Val,

you are dead!
monday after
school at your
house. I warn
you, you better
not have any
friends over,
because if I
hit you I don't
want people on
my back. I
won't bring
friends
neither.

you better
write back
telling me
the answer.

P.s I told
kim to leave
you alone
because I
want something
to wack.

"Daggers through my soul,
Stakes through my heart.
All this I could bear,
But not us being apart.
Life without you is like
living without food & water.
None of that matters now.
I'll feel I'm losing touch
with reality. I'll never
get back. Tell me you don't
hate me and don't lie. I
can't go on without you.
Life means no more for
me. I feel like I'm dead
and maybe without you
I am. I'm robbed of my
soul and my heart. My
emotions flow free. I give
up."

Dear Always,

A page goes by; a day goes by.
My life's "used to be" just isn't.
Things change, People grow, yet most don't.
I change everyday, though I may feel the same
Never a dull moment in my deep, dark, tortured soul.
Maybe someday I'll change, maybe not, who knows.
Depressing, post-apocalyptic thoughts out my pen flow.
My eyes, though they see, are blind to some things.
Never a day goes by I don't feel the same emotions.
Love unrequited; never spoken of, never had, never been.
Friends gone past, ever-forgotten, always loved.
Promises never broken, doors left hanging open
Always the kinds of things most discuss freely.
Keep 'em stifled, don't take chances, she won't go for it.
Self-damage kept in a can in a dark, locked room.
Maybe someday; maybe someday, always my answer.
How the Hell do I do this? I know it won't
work, it'll only end in tradegy; just you
wait, I told you so. You are unloved,
and you are meant to stay that way,
boy! Just remember that. Alone,
Alone, Alone, with a capital a.
don't even try to escape. Never.
Never.
Always?

Dear Always * Brian Byrne

Most research on clinical depression indicates that the condition begins to surface in one's late teens and early twenties. I am now in my early thirties, and have learned enough about myself since I wrote this, at age eighteen, to know that it probably wouldn't have been the worst idea to have some controlling medical authority begin dosing me with industrial-grade antidepressants at about this time. Ideally this would have taken place a few months before I put pen to paper and, in handwriting worthy of a fourth-grade penmanship award, refer to "my tortured soul" without one single milligram of irony.

I mean, one of several really remarkable things about this—what in God's name is this, anyway? prose? a poem? a prose poem? a prosaic poem?—is that, while I clearly had the wherewithal to commit this peppy little number to paper, I was categorically unqualified to do so in any capacity, other than the fact that I owned (a) a pen and (b) at least one sheet of paper. (At a glance, I think it's not unfair to speculate that the length of this thing probably had a lot to do with a desire to fill, yet not exceed, a single page in a notebook.) No, seriously, listen: I'm pretty sure that when I wrote this, I'd finished reading fewer than five full-length novels that did not prominently feature Ramona Quimby. Also, "fewer than five" may kinda be padding things a little. It should go without saying that I hadn't come within about thirty feet of much actual poetry, either. So what literary influences shaped this missive to "Always"?

A brief accounting:
- The writing staff at Marvel Comics, circa 1986–1993
- Dave Barry, humor columnist
- The collected works of countless prime-time network sitcom writers
- Professional lyricists including, but not limited to: W. Axl Rose,

Dear Always, cont.

Sebastian Bach, James Hetfield, Jani Lane, Michael Patton, Sammy Hagar, David Lee Roth, Gary Cherone, and the guy from Ugly Kid Joe, who I later found out did not actually write "Cat's in the Cradle," but whose work still apparently resonated on some level

Will the reader be particularly surprised to hear the author describe his eighteen-year-old self as big and kinda dumpy, with a poorly maintained ponytail, a black trench coat, and not one but two (2) of those Rastafarian hats? I think maybe not so much. Has the reader assumed from the get-go that this page of introspection was the result of some unrequited crush or another? I would be flabbergasted if the reader had not.

Beyond that, I believe "Dear Always" pretty much speaks for itself. *"Always?"*

Jesus Roosevelt Christ. Here's to being old.

Why Why Why Why Why Why
Why Why Why Why Why Why
Why Why Why Why Why
Why Why Why Why Why Why
Why Why Why Why Why Why
Why Why Why Why Why Why
Why Why Why Why Why Why
Why Why Why Why Why
Why Why Why Why Why
Why Why Why Why Why
Why Why Why Why Why
Why Why Why Why Why
Why Why Why Why Why Why
Why Why Why Why Why
Why Why Why Why Why
Why Why Why Why Why
Why Why Why Why Why
Why Why Why Why Why
Why Why Why Why
Why Why Why Why Why
Why Why Why Why
Why Why Why Why
Why Why Why Why
Why Why Why Why Why
Why Why Why Why Why
Why Why Why Why
Why Why Why Why
Why Why Why Why

eight
hundred
and
seventy
one
questions
why
is
this
so
heart
beats
within
me
only
to
prolong
the
search
why
did
it
happen
soul
aches

within
me
only
to
prolong
the
pain
of
questions
that
will
go
unanswered
for
eight
hundred
and
seventy
one
lifetimes
why
is
this
so

Company
Made in Brazil

Editor's Note:

This has to be a code. What's the significance of eight hundred and seventy one? Da Vinci? Freemasons? Illuminati? Most likely the first part of a certain someone's phone number.

In Pensive Mood I Wandered Afar
* Jennifer Boyer

Anne Frank inspired me to name all my journals, which is why this entry is addressed to a person. Because, after all, the petulant woes of a middle-class American teen are so similar to those of a Jewish girl forced into years of terrifying, ratlike hiding by a genocidal regime.

   I was fifteen when I wrote this entry; I thought I was terribly "deep" and had an "old soul" because I halfheartedly worried about the plight of Romanians and Ethiopians. But not enough to actually, like, donate my allowance to them, mind you.

June 20, 1989   Tuesday
Arrie,
I took a walk under cloudy ~~skies~~ and
Threatening skies just now, "In pensive
mood I wandered afar," I guess you
could say. A drop of rain fell down, and
touched my eye, but evaporated before it
could slide down my cheek, like a tear. And
then I got to thinking, you know, about
the sky; how beyond the clouds the sun
still shone, and how it's the same sky
which is all over the world at this
moment. It covers London, my precious
London, Paris, Rome, Romania, Czechoslovakia;
over the dying in Ethiopia, and those who
live in New York City. Somewhere, caught
in between, in a small corner of Pennsylvania,
wanders a lonely girl, lost in thought,
under that same sky. Maybe the whole
sky is God, looking down upon all of us
at once, choosing mercy for some, and misery
for others. Those who love life have it
grabbed from them, and those who loathe
it are kept hanging on until they destroy
themselves. Who am I?
                              ~ Jennifer

14 February 1991 Wednesday

Emma,

I'm so nuts, now. I can't handle any of this shit. I wish I was dead, dead, dead. Everything is just entirely too much. All I've been living for lately is to have monday off to relax, to veg out ... and now we've got an all-day rehersal, plus one on Saturday. I was so upset I lost my monday I almost cried. All this musical, quiz bowl, working with grades... I can't handle it. I just can't. And everyone in the halls gets me scared. Today I got up from my seat in Latin and the guy behind me said rudely. "She always cuts in front of me"! Then I go out into the hallway and Amy Kern bumps into me and laughs. Then I'm walking to Humanities with Missy and she gets bitchy and says, "why can't you die?" and I say, "yes, why can't I?" I feel so at odds with everyone. If only I could just lay down and die, or disappear. Oh Emma... I don't have any more strength. I'm a puppet atoss in the masses. My mind is numb with a million pressing needs. There's nothing here but nothing. I just want to go home, crawl underneath my bed, listen to Puccini and renounce it all. Maybe I will. maybe... I

There's Nothing Here But Nothing

Jonathan Boyd

Well, Happy Valentine's Day 1991 to me! This entry perfectly illustrates an equation that even a math idiot like myself can understand: severe clinical depression + 16-year-old angst + self-absorption = overwrought histrionics.

I love how trivial things like quiz bowl and my high school musical rehearsals (as compared to, say, the Gulf War, which took place one month earlier) were the last straw—the catalyst for me crawling beneath my bed, weeping to the sounds of a Puccini tape, and renouncing it all.

The Burden of Constant Pondering * Jen Bandini

Much like Anne Frank, I've always understood the importance of my work to future generations. I mean, I was the *only* angst-ridden and alienated middle-class white teenage girl in '80s/'90s America, right? This "piece" is the introduction to one of my many "works" under way and is pretty much self-explanatory. It makes me want to puke a little. My favorite part is the reference to my other "book" with its endlessly creative and original title, "Silent All These Years," which is the id to this ego. Am I still this pompous?

April 5, 1993

When someday some unknown person comes
across my many writings, he or she will be much
confused by the manner in which I created
them, for I have several different notebooks,
each of which serve a seperate purpose. As
one book, "Silent All These Years," is coming
near its end, I am faced with deciding whether
it is still a necessary part of my life. In that
book, I vent all my emotions — anger, loneliness,
resentment, jealousy and even a small amount of
joy — and and I have not yet determined
whether I need to do so still, for my emotions
seem to have run dry for a short time. Instead,
I have turned to thought, simple thought, to
spend my time. (Reincarnation being the subject
which has most recently occupied my mind.)
And so I have this new book in which to set
them down for all to read (in the future... who
care to read, I should say), and my mind may
rest in having eased itself of the burden
of its constant ponderings. More of it all tomorrow!

100%
GRADE A
BITCH

III.

You could have been my savior, like
    Jesus or MLK.
Instead, you ran away.
And I have nothing to say
~~but for~~ your name.
Shame.
Your tongue a flame
    that burned my moaning skin.
I let you in.
The sin was sweet.
But you grew bitter—dark, like the street
    on which I stood and screamed your name, in pain,
In vain.
This bed on which you've lain
    still bears your stain.

AS MANY GO
TO HELL
AS HEAVEN

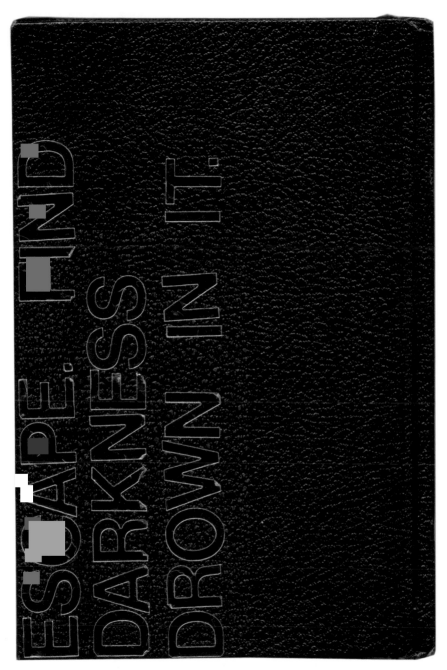

ESCAPE. FIND
DARKNESS IN IT.
DROWN IN IT.

I remember asking a friend if the back of my journal seemed too melodramatic, and she politely replied, "Well, maybe just a little." I didn't talk to her for two days.

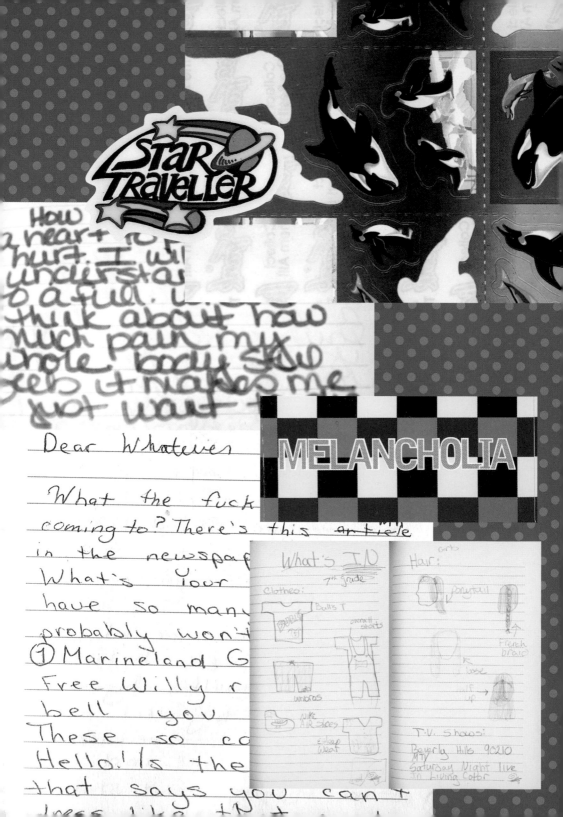

STAR TRAVELLER

HOW
a heart to
hurt. I wil
understa
o a full. C
think about how
much pain my
whole body slow
feels it makes me
just want t

Dear Whatever

MELANCHOLIA

What the fuck
coming to? There's this article
in the newspap
What's your
have so many
probably won't
① Marineland G
Free Willy r
bell you
These so co
Hello! Is the
that says you can't
dress like that

What's IN
7th grade
Clothes:
Bulls T
overall shorts
umbros
NIKE
AIR shoes
deep
wear

Hair: arts
ponytail
French
braid
loose
up → up

T.V. shows:
Beverly Hills 90210
MTV
Saturday Night Live
In Living Color

June 6, 1991

I did it- I had sex with
_ho!!! ❤!! Holy shit. I can't
I'm not a virgin anymore.
know where to start.
so cool to say it, or

am the main character
of a big movie that
isn't being filmed,
but is happening
on the movie
screen as soon
we act it out.
I don't know any
of the lines so
I just do what
happens. They
other main
character, (why
I don't know)
is

George Micheal. We
are supposed
to save some
5 year old chourus
singer at Frav-
enstein. It's like
a jungle and
we ride on the
same horse and
we are great
swords people.
We ca
cha   getting
it

-fan mail-

5 Buddies and Death Threats

Frien

d s

Before puberty, your friendships typically spring from who lives next door and how cool their Legos are. Once puberty hits, though, your friendships take on a deeper significance. You become blood brothers. You make secret pacts. You weather Shakespearean betrayals. You fight like lovers, like siblings, like enemies. You can't decide if you want to be best friends, or if you hate them.

When you get to the point where your friendships are the largest source of drama and turmoil in your life, that's a pretty good indication that you're finally ready to start dating.

Dear Pam,   4/80/1

I feel very dumb writing you because I know you probably don't even remember me. But if you remember Fiedel Camp I think you'll remember me. I'm your best friend from Camp. We tried to But a Snack Bar but failed. You Hated Kim Bernstein. I'm Alice Bradley from Group #18. Hi!!! The reason I'm writing is not a happy one. Everything seems so strange. Nothing is going right any more. All my friends are moving. My one friend, Lynn Kochendonfor is driving me crazy! She repeats everything I say, acts silly all the time, hang-ing on me then she ins-ults me by telling me to get out of my seat so my other friend, Michelle, can sit there. Then every-

Hello there!

day she asks me if I can come over her house. I can't say no anymore. (I bet you think I'm just a compla-iner. Well, I'm not. I just need someone to talk to.) I feel alone and confused. No one wants to be serious anymore. They just dream things instead of doing them. That's why I want to do something. I want to forget everything I've said, to tell off my friends, and begin a new life. All my friends think I'm a lunatic! Every single time my friends say something they mumble it. I ask them to speak louder and they say "forget it" and they look at me like I'm kind of crazy person. But forget all that. I hope you write to me. I would really like it if you called me. My Phone Number is 628—

I Think You'll Remember Me, I'm Your Best Friend * Alice Bradley

I vividly recall the night that I wrote this letter, which is weird, because I don't remember much else about being a tortured eleven-year-old. Shortly after pouring my heart out to Pam, I joined my family downstairs. They were watching a television special about the 1980s, starring the *Three's Company* cast. I'm not sure what the point of the show was, except that previous decades were hilarious (especially when reenacted by John Ritter et al.), and the 1980s would be doubly so. I was watching television with my family, my sister was home from college, and then—THEN!—my mom walked in with homemade caramel custard. How could I stay depressed?

Sometime after I decided not to send the letter, my mother found it, pocketed it, and saved it for two decades, waiting for the right opportunity to spring it on me. For twenty years, she probably periodically took it out of her sock drawer, read it, and cackled. She's a good cook, but a cruel, cruel woman.

This page (this page only) will
be about Christi Edwards,
what I hate about her!

started
4/11/87

1. went through my spiral, tore
everything out, threw it away,
and let mother have the
spiral
2. "You're not supposed to look in
other people's refrigerators."
3. Told me Daryle calls her <u>all</u>
the time.
4. Says she never farts
5. Prissy
6. Said Lorie was ugly

The We Hate Christi Edwards Club
* Tracy Carr

I started this list in eighth grade, when I was actually friends with Christi
Edwards, but later in the school year three other girls and I formed the
WHCEC: the We Hate Christi Edwards Club. By the end of the school year
my conscience—the existence of which was obviously debatable—showed
up, and I wrote Christi Edwards an apology note. We became friends
again, and later she made out with a boy I liked, but I deserved it. Also, to
be fair, Lorie WAS pretty ugly in those days.

STUDENT
OF THE
MONTH

**TRACIE
MASEK**

**GRADE
6**

The Notebook of Rage and Hatred
* Tracie Masek

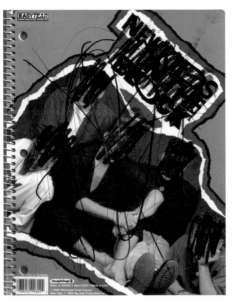

When I was a kid, I'd say between the ages of nine and twelve, I kept a Notebook of Rage and Hatred, which I used to express my anger toward other people. Anytime someone would really piss me off, I'd run upstairs to my bedroom and pull out my notebook and scribble something mean about them to make myself feel better. I started with the New Kids on the Block, who had severely let me down when they suddenly turned very not-cool, and then, you know, Donnie burnt down that hotel or whatever.

Brennon Williams: Brennon Williams was the first friend I made when we moved to Ohio in kindergarten, and I have no idea what he might have done to me to so offend my sense of justice. Brennon is one of the nicest people in the world. Guess he was a little turd when he was younger.

Kelan Williams: Kelan, Brennon's little brother, stood up on the bus and announced that Santa Claus wasn't real in front of my little sister, who was distraught. I told Megan that Kelan was lying, and he was just jealous because he was a Jehovah's Witness and didn't get to celebrate Christmas.

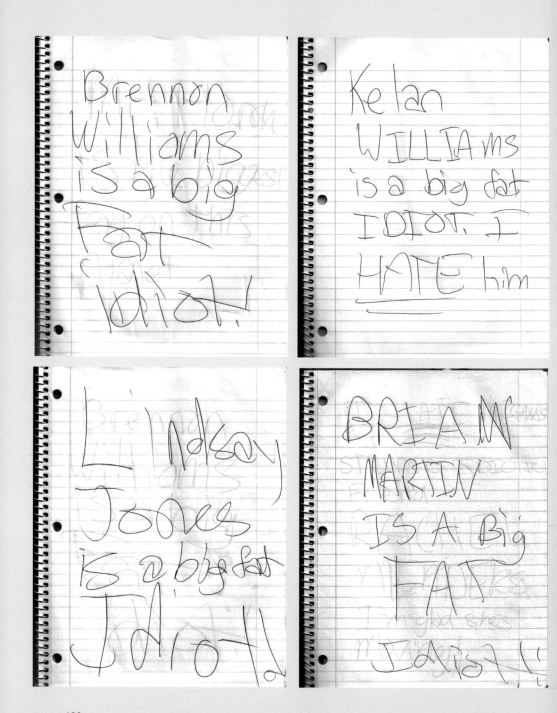

108

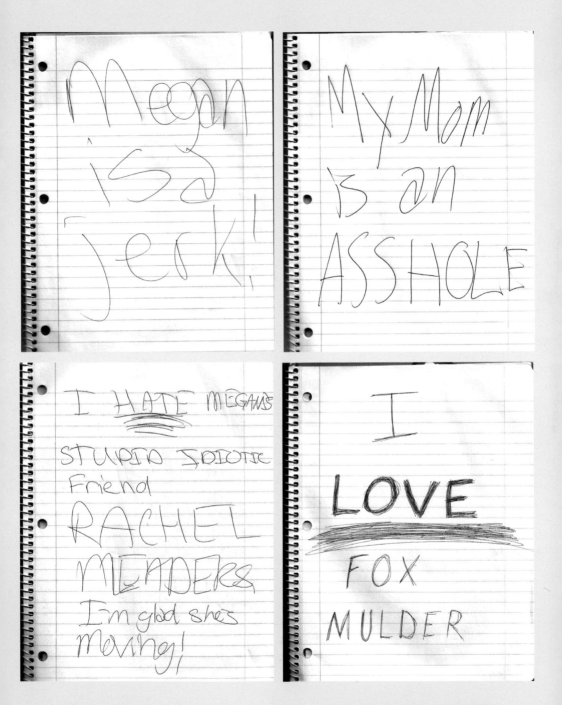

109

Lindsay Jones: Lindsay is my cousin, and we get along really well now, but we used to sort of hate each other when we were younger. I'm not sure why. Although it might have something to do with that time we both ran for mayor of our fake town, and I won the election, and Lindsay was the town dog instead.

Brian Martin: To the best of memory, Brian Martin was a big fat idiot.

Megan: Anger doesn't necessarily translate into poetry. Megan's my sister. That sort of explains it.

Mom: Ooooh! First cussword! Also, note the pre-Internet use of capitalization to denote shouting.

Rachel Meaders: Rachel Meaders was the most annoying girl ever. I am glad she moved.

Mom and Dad are buttheads: I think this is my favorite. I'm sure I got in trouble for talking back and somehow having worked the word *No* into my smart-ass routine. Go sit on a pin! Zing!

Fox Mulder: Apparently, there was some room in the Notebook of Rage and Hatred for a little love. This is still so embarrassing to me that I can't stand to look directly at it.

My mom and Dad are buttheads and this is what I say to them... NO NO NO NO NO NO NO!

To Rita.   October 16/81
I'm real sorry about writing that note. Do me
a favour burn it. I'm sorry a guy made me mad at you.
I understand why you need someone I've had Ronny and
Bruce. I hope you get him. I needed A guy because I'm
sick of sitting with everyone at lunch and in class and
them talking about guys. I always have nothing to say.
Now they always ask everyone but me who they
like. I feel so out of place with everyone.
    Your my best friend now and I hope it will
always stay this way. I never want anything like
a guy to upset us. I hope you think the same. Please
come to the dance. that way if we don't dance we'll
each have a best friend to talk too.

                    Traci

    P.S. I don't know what I'm going to do about boarding school.
My mom says if my report card is bad I'm going no
matter what. I know I've done bad in french, science,
and I don't know.
    If I ever had to leave I'd miss having a best
friend around to talk to and keep me out of troble.

Do Me a Favor, Burn It * Rita Schepok

Traci and I were best friends beginning in elementary school. I was a bit of a late bloomer and her first foray into boys when we hit ninth grade was making me feel a bit left out and jealous. From what I remember, the event that inspired this note was a crush we both had on the same guy, and an argument about who should get him. She seems to have decided I deserved him because she already "had" Ronny and Bruce. The guy must have been quite something, because I have no idea who he was and ultimately neither of us "got" him. Oh, and incidentally, Traci did end up going to boarding school for a few years.

Traci and I still live on the same street and continue to be good friends to this day, more than twenty-five years after the note was written.

Death Threats * Brad Walsh

Ray was my best friend in high school (a uniformed, all-boys' private school in the middle of the woods in Ohio), and the only friend from that school whom I still talk to today. We were completely different; the only thing that made us similar was that we were both so awkward. Today I'm a photographer in New York, and he's an accountant in Akron.

I kept a journal at that time mostly because I felt I should. One of my friends' mothers once told me that when I was older, I would be very happy to have kept a journal during these years. But rather than document the bullshit that goes along with being gay in an all-boys' high school and

hiding relationships that happened under the tables during English class, most of what I wrote about were coded desires, my dreams, and the stupid things that Ray and I did to each other. We left death threats in each other's mailboxes. Waited around after concerts to try to meet bands I don't even remember anymore. Made bets on who played the lead in the movie we just sat through. We hit each other a lot.

What those journals are good for today is to remind me when I think I'm hot shit, that, in fact, I'm probably the biggest idiot that I have known—or at least I'm in the top two. But they also serve to contradict me today when I say that high school sucked; these prove that I had a good friend, and a lot of good times.

I am still giving Ray Death threats and he still has no idea who is sending them. i put a typed note in his mailbox and a picture of a black rose, And then an hour later he comes back to me saying "somebody keeps leaving me death threats in my mailbox!" the first one i did was put the death card (tarot card) in his box, which really freaked him out. I can't believe he doesn't know its me, how stupid can he be? I'm the only one who ever pays attention to him. But ~~then~~ then again he is the one who bet me $20 it was Sharon Stone in ~~Deep~~ Impact. What an idiot.

we hugged.
it was like
we were old friends.
even in the dream i didn't
know her, though.

Becky and Ray and I
played truth or Dare for
no real Reason and we
all ended up w/ no clothes
on at all and Becky
did something horrible.

Ray left us when me and Helen
were at the table with him and
Nicole because he was nervous. I figured
he was going to the bathroom because
he has a nervous stomach like my
mom. But he was gone for like half
an hour. Nicole started getting mad at me
because she was sitting by herself the
whole time, and when I went ~~all~~
looking for Ray I found him in the
lobby. He was talking on the payphone
with his best friend in Hawaii with his
shirt unbuttoned and his stomach
all hanging out. He was scratching
his stomach and fanning his shirt open
at the front door and I knew he
got hives when he was nervous. I
asked him what he was doing and all
he said was "I'm on the phone to
Hawaii". He told me today that he
didn't want to be itching himself in
front of Nicole because she would think
that was gross. But when I took him
back to the table he spilled a candle on
Helen anyway so the girls loaded it with
him.
        Oh, and I told him I left

the death cash in his box, and
that made him so mad.!

ASK MR Reader
If 3-26 IS
Still Missing

April 14, 1992

Dear Journal,

Emma is upset with me. We used to be lovers, but now it's different. We broke up! I'm soo sad. All those times, just gone. She said that it wouldn't effect our relationship as friends any, but I know that it will. Emma is my best buddy, and now we aren't. ████ wrote me a letter, and her father abuses her and her mother. I am so scared for both of them. Kerri didn't get me a present from Mexico, and she got all her other friends one. Today hasn't been a good day, at all points.

~Maggie

my 6th grade school picture!

Today Hasn't Been a Good Day, At All Points * Maggie Jacobstein

Emily and Kate were my best friends in the sixth grade. Apparently we were also "lovers." As I recall, all this meant was that we were very "dedicated" to one another. I am aware now of how strange it must have been for Emily and Kate to have such terminology applied to our innocent (and platonic) relationship.

I recently spoke to Emily, read her the entry, and told her that I had been reading this—along with the rest of my diary—in public and she promptly hung up the phone. When I called back and said, "It was so nice talking to you, let's talk soon again!" she said, "Ummm . . . yes, Maggie. But please don't read that anymore. I don't want my husband to get the wrong idea." Do you think she'll mind me putting it in a book?

april 14, 1992 (cont.)

I made up with Emmy! Kate, Emily, and I all decided to just cool off this whole relationship thing. It is causing to much tension. Kate said that I should tell ████ to tell an adult about what is happening at home. I'm so so scared for her. I really like sex diff. It is probaly just a stage of puberty. I hate when my mom talks about things like that with me. Well I'm tired, so bye!

Mags

As far as Kerri not bringing me a present from Mexico, I'm still mad. I hope she sees this and feels bad.

to impress. I won't put all
my secrets in now because
then I won't have any later.

Love,
Maggie

P.S. I can't believe I forgot to
tell you what I did so here goes.
Tonight I went to a violin
contrato. It was kind-a boring.
~~But stupid~~

Dear Diary,
Today I am mad for
~~red~~ ~~two~~ reasons.
Number one, my doll
won't go to the ba-
room. Number Two
~~I~~ I lost my gold loc
Number Three Jenifa
didn't call ~~please~~
loud enough for
me to hear but
loud enough for
cindy to hear so
she can steel the

I ♥ D

JAMES

still here! I miss
him so much. If
he was here again
I wouldnt even
hesitate to ask
him to dance. Oh
well no use in dwelling

XXXXTER

H ♥ D

WHATEVER

WHATEVER

1993

How to be a Vamp

VAMPISM

visuals

1. anti-sun poster
2. sun hat
3. all black clot
4. guidelines

Long Ago and far away
in the October of 1990.
students by
Kiyomi Nogu
earthshatter
the increasin

young pioneers'
This was no
way to up
and

P.S.
I love you

I ♥
YOU

6 I Don't Like You

Love

Teenage love isn't so much about happiness; it's about longing and plotting and heartbreak and revenge. It's about reading monumental clues into tiny actions. It's never about being together; it's always about being apart. It's about confusion. It's about misery. This makes teenage love *so good*.

The Face That Launched My Bicycle
* Jessica Wiseman

I met him the summer after I turned fifteen. My hair was big (though never, I felt, quite big enough), and my mouth full of braces. How I fell so hard and obsessed for so long is still kind of a mystery. Nathan was kind to me despite my obvious and surely pathetic besottment, but we never had a

relationship, not even one you could call a friendship, really. We were mere acquaintances, yet I wore out the sidewalk in front of his house walking or biking past hoping for just a glimpse of his blond hair and shocking blue eyes. I even hid in his bushes with my giggling girlfriends, and nearly died if I happened to see his dad. Because hello, that man got to live with and see the one I knew I loved every single day, and how lucky was he?

When a friend of mine found a pile of old yearbooks in the school library, I cried like those girls you see in old footage of the Beatles performing. I photocopied all of the pictures I could find of him and created this love collage. I'm not going to tell you that I kissed it every night before I went to bed, because that would be, you know, embarrassing.

To the face that launched my bicycle countless times,

I think of you and cry. I think of you and smile. I think of you laugh. I think of you and scream. I think of you and jump up and down. I think of you and want to see you again. I think of you and wonder, do you think of me too? I pray, I hope, I dream & fantisize. I love you more than words can say. Lust? No, because I know you are worthy of the kingdom of heaven. I am trying to be worthy & follow your example. Worldly temptations only scare me, that if I did something like that - I know I would loose you forever. I envy the woman you marry, for surely she will be beautiful, unlike me and probably smarter, but will she be worthy of you? I know I'm not. I could never even hope for a prize such as you. I love you with all my heart.

Love, Jessica
yours faithfuly always

Everything Has Changed * Tracy Carr

I am not sure how "a long curly tail" and "new wave" go together, but in 1987 it made a lot of sense. The best part about this guy giving me a note and a tape is that he came up to me in the hall and said, "Do you have a Spuds MacKenzie shirt?" I lied and said no. I love that that was the big test, and that I knew enough to lie to a cool guy.

This is me at the time I was fascinated by "major N.W.s." You can see why I would be impressed.

September
September

It's September 5, and everything has changed! yay! I thought Daryle was a new dawer, but oh my goodness, Shannon's a major n.w. Shannon is fine! He has sticking up straight hair, a long curly tail and glasses. HE IS A JUNIOR! I am a freshman! He likes me, I think. He gave me a tape and a note and the note said to call him! Yesterday I did! He's so SWEET & weird! He called me back that day! Today I called Kim & we talked about the SAT.

My Dearest Aubrey,

Yes, I know you like me but I just want you to know that — I don't like you and I'm not gonna ask you out! To me you are annoying so stop making my life a living hell. Sorry to disappoint you! Just stop calling me, writing me notes and bugging me. Basically, I'm trying to say LEAVE ME THE HELL ALONE! However, I mean that in the nicest way possibly. It's just I don't want to go out with anyone. Well, I have better things to do than write you.

P.S. So how'd you like my first+last note!

Love,
Nick

Let's still be friends

Let's Still Be Friends * Aubrey Sabala

I liked him. I thought he liked me . . . he used to meet me at my locker and walk with me to our classes. He was cute and charming in that hadn't-yet-hit-puberty sort of way. It was the era of passing notes, and alas, I apparently sent him one or two and was hoping he would send me one back. He did . . . just not exactly what I was looking for. My favorite part is that the outside of this note said, "Howdy Babe!"

I wonder what ever happened to him, and if he still wants to be friends.

Say It with Puffy Paint · Lori Dalton

Reading this now makes me want to crawl under the dining-room table and die. (But not before pointing out my somewhat-abstract depiction of eyelashes and tears next to the dated song reference.) I had a crush on

DAY Wednesday   DATE November 16, 1988
        Today was one of the worst
days of my life. I don't know
how to explain See, this morning
Matt ████ comes up to me and says,"
I've got some bad news. Andy doesn't want
to go out." At 1st I think he's kidding.
Then I realize he's not, I'm to
stunned to talk, (or think.) All day I've
thought about him. But remember before

DAY_____   DATE_____
    I wrote I'm not giving up til I
go out with him. Well I'm not, Or
at least until I find out why
Andy doesn't want to. So I've got
to talk to Matt tomorrow. It
just better not be some lame
excuse. If it's just what he's afraid
of asking, then I'll ask him out!!
I'd do anything for him.

Andy for the better part of seventh grade. Despite my best efforts, however, the closest we ever got was a few slow dances at a classmate's Bat Mitzvah. This resulted in hours of free time in which I learned to suffer for my art and ultimately construct my inspired series of "I Heart Andy" graffiti pieces in Neon Puffy Paint on Canvas Keds, Plastic Toiletries, © 1988.

DAY cont   DATE

He was sick on Monday, and that nite I prayed For him. I actually prayed for him to gett better! Now I almost wish I didn't, because he couldt have stayed home today & this awful day wouldn't have happened.

But I love Andy so much, more than I could ever say! I mean I wrote "I ♡ ANDY" on

DAY   DATE

my toothbrushes with puffy paint! (And on my KEDS, which Josh showed to him!) Now come on!

I can't wait for tomorrow, & find out what's going on. I'll keep you posted.

P.S.
IF I hear kind of groovy love "J ''I cry

131

Ringgg.... Click....

"Hey Steve! This is Krissy. Remember me? Well, I got picked as a recruiter for the Crop Walk and I'm supposed to get people from G.U. congregation to sign up. Would you be interested? If you are, I could give you the forms at church - but you never come, so I'll just give them to Melinda at school and she can pass them on to you. Oh - do you want to bring a friend to the walk? I'll give Melinda a form for herself, too, then!... How am I? Oh great, fantastic! Ever since you broke my heart my life has been going super! And it really made me happy when Lori said she saw you + Melinda making out! Boy! I'm so lucky! Well, I've really got to call some other people + you're probably getting ready to go out with Melinda, right? What - oh, she's over there now? Oh neat! Be sure and tell her I said hi and I'll see her at school! O.K. great. Bye Bye! (you asshole)"

slam

Ever Since You Broke My Heart, My Life Has Been Going Super! * Kristine Smith

This guy had been my first date. I was fourteen and he was eighteen, but his family went to my church so my parents said it was OK. He took me to see *The Outsiders* and to Pizza Hut. He also came over to watch TV once. That was it. But really, psycho-possessiveness doesn't need much to hold on to, you know? This was a fantasy phone call to him after he dropped me.

The worst part is that this phone call was only a fantasy.

The best part is that this phone call was only a fantasy.

"Cirkers 5717" * Danielle Henderson

Once Lou Reed taught me that poems didn't have to rhyme, I was off and running. The title probably references the bus seat number and manufacturer's name, as was my style in those idealistic days of traveling home from college during my freshman year ("Taco Bell Order #49" is another prolific ballad). It reads like I want to hold this guy down and forcibly cuddle. "Put the Lotion in the Basket, Kyle" was a working title.

Cirkers 5717

I find myself thinking of you
at the most improbable times;
You-
Whom I have only experienced a
thin sliver of
Yet have known of you for what
Seems like an eon.
And isn't it amazing how one
mere minute can feel like
An eternity?
Sometimes,
with some people,
it can be just that way;
a lifetime passed between
a glance.
A glance.
Your gaze spoke so much
to me, for whatever reason.
The expressiveness of your
face not soon to be lost.
And I see within you a
vulnerability that makes
me want to reach out and hold
you, despite the harsh front and
jagged words you present to others.

Am I wrong to feel this way?
Was someone right in saying
that I move things too fast
(or was that someone me)?
I cannot be bothered by
Such things —

All I know is that
I long to know you,
To find out all of your
quirks,
To envelope you in
kindness and to
ultimately be your
friend.

— written for Kyle on a bus
to Lasell College; turns
out he had a girlfriend
anyway. 1996

Monday   September 23, 1991
    I'm sorry. I just have to tell
you about last night. Last night
Pete & I went to sleep together on
the phone. Lemme 'splain. We'd
been talking about doing that for
a while, like how awesome it
would be if we could wake up
& have the first thing we hear
is each other. It was awesome.
Last night we talked til about
10 of 1, then we just held the
phones by our ears & went to
sleep. It was so cool knowing
that the person we care most
about is right there if anything
happened. He woke me up at
4:50 & we talked for a couple
minutes b4 going back to bed. Then
my alarm went off a couple seconds
before his, & b4 he could even
think I was just like Hi Pete. We
might do it again tonight - I
don't know. But I do know that
that wasn't the last time!

Pete-n-Lori BFF * Lori Dalton

This entry still makes my heart sigh a bit. Pete was my first true love; within days of meeting, we became best friends and dated for nine months during my sophomore and his junior year of high school. We were each other's "last call" before bed, and one night, we decided that we just didn't want to hang up the phone. We synchronized our alarm clocks to wake us up the next morning, and after saying goodnight, set our phone receivers down alongside our beds. It was like having each other there in the room, but of course, we lived across town.

We did this every night for eight months or so, until my mom bought a new phone for her bedroom that lit up whenever another extension was in use. She woke up one night, saw the light on, and it just seemed easier to stop rather than have to explain why Pete and I did this. We had started falling out of love by that point, anyway, and it seemed like a convenient way of letting things go, bit by bit, until we broke up a month later.

We Will Survive, Won't We? * Kitty Joe Sainte-Marie

Yeah, I thought Eli and I were total soul mates, perfection. I thought we had a bond unbroken by petty things or even terrible and huge discrepancies in our lifestyles,—*like him being gay.* No biggie.

Classic scenario, right? Closeted gay boyfriend (yes, I knew he was gay the moment I laid eyes on his pretty face—so no excuses for that brilliant decision!) implores you to seek other men so he can (a) live vicariously through you, begging for every lurid detail and (b) be relieved of the arduous task of fulfilling your "needs." The whole mess backfires when, shockingly, you fall in love with the man who actually loves your breasts and wants more than wardrobe advice from you. Yet, leaving the gay boyfriend and the life of martyrdom you signed up for equals the apocalypse. Aren't open relationships supposed to be simple and free?!

We will survive, won't we? Um. No.

huddled up on the bathroom talking to parker - everything clear. everything wonderful - my path laid out by the simple following of my heart. my active heart lead me to parker, to a relationship that is whole and fulfilling, to someone who is ready to love me and only me. someone who is fulfilled by me. i need it.

my dying heart cries in pain. my eli heart is tough has been stabbed and gouged and beaten down, scars and stitches, bandaid and casts. it insists it can endure this half love that eli gives me. but i must slay it.

another day. another life. another tear is hitting my page.

someday eli will be ready to love me. and i'll be ready again to love him. i was there waiting but the train never came. so along comes parker. i am lucky to have captivated him, as he calls it. he loves me more daily, ecstatic to know me more; love me more, make me smile.

i held eli, sweet eli all night feeling his sleep, his soul rest, bracing his heart and holding mine to his back. we will survive, won't we?

PAST LOVES:
if i can remember dem all!
or if dem will all fit!

KRISTA VON. SLOAN

HANAUGTCH LEVITT

AMY BIERMANN

LEAH MCKELVEY

LARA PROEGLER

MELLISA BOLLMAN

ABBY ALWIN

JASMINE O'CONNOES

SUSIE ATKINS

KALI MALORY-MEDWED

SARAH BEAUDREAU

TERRA DIONNE

ALLISON FABER

COLLEEN ERNST

JENNY SPEARS

JAVI BENAVENTE

ERIN BARCLAY

SARAH JACOLBY

TANYA POHRT

CAILIN CAMMAN

HEIDI KNAB

KATY CROSBY

THE FUTURE

THE FARTHER FUTURE

The Further Future * Davy Rothbart

What makes you cringe the most, I think, when you look through your childhood journals, are those moments when you realize how little you've changed.

I made this list of the twenty-three loves of my life when I was twelve years old. Most of them I'd never even spoken to. I'd never gone on a date with any of them. There'd never been a kiss. (A decade later, I did make out with one lucky lady among them for a few minutes in the alleyway outside the 8 Ball Saloon.)

It's been twenty years, and I still fall in love with people I'm too afraid to talk to and will never meet. The further future, I see, is now.

Are You in for a Surprise!
* Blaise Kearsley

In 1987, at age fourteen, I fell truly, madly, deeply in love. Three times. In the span of about four weeks. First, my boyfriend Mark, to whom I was completely devoted, dumped me over the phone one night right after an episode of *Growing Pains*. His primary reason was that we never got to see each other because of "transportation and parent problems." While I was reeling from that unbearable heartbreak, I met Wade, who looked exactly like River Phoenix, but with braces. My love affair with Wade lasted seven days, which was just enough time to completely get over Mark, and to become totally in love with Mark's best friend, Jonah. This was a love like no other I'd known. Not even the ones I'd had just a few weeks earlier.

Dear Diary,   Saturday, January 31, 1987

    I woke up to find my eyes were all swollen and bloodshot from bawling
the night before. When I went to the mirror the first thing that greeted
me, besides myself, was the small picture of Mark taped to the corner.
Well, let me tell you, seeing his blonde, gorgeous self smiling at me like
that really hurt. I got to school at 7:45. No one was in homeroom yet and
I had the emptiest, deepest feeling inside me. I couldn't believe it was
over. I felt empty with sadness, but full of despair at the same time.
What really bothers me is that he said he had been thinking about breaking
up with me for a couple of weeks. But just last Saturday we were having an
incredibly intense conversation. "Nothing lasts forever" I said (being my
realistic, practical self). "You shouldn't say that," he replied. "My
love for you will last forever. My love for you will never die." How could
he say those things to me while thinking about dumping me at the same
time? There was only one way—BULLSHIT. Words cannot describe how much I
loved Mark. God only knows how he felt about me. God's the only one who
knows. Actually, he's not. There are two people: God and Mark's sister
Amy. THAT BITCH!
    About the whole "Wade thing," I'm kind of happy about it but not
really into it. (For obvious reasons.) He asked me if I was going out with
anyone and I said I had just broken up with my boyfriend. Wade read me
poems he wrote when he was eight years old. One was called "The Lovebird
Who Couldn't Smile." The other one was called "The Autobiography of Wade
Reynolds." They were so adorable.

                                                          March 28th

Dear Diary,
    HA! HA! HA! ARE YOU IN FOR A SURPRISE!!!! Jonah and I are going out! He
had been calling me faithfully every single day after school and one thing
sort of just led to another. My first date with Jonah was March 7th. I was
really nervous. He was wearing beige, baggy pants, a Velvet Underground
T-shirt, a jeans jacket, and this AWESOME hat that he told me about over the
phone. We did fool around but we only went to second. It was hard for me to
get used to the way that Jonah kisses. At first I didn't like it. At two
points we were lying on the floor and at one point we were standing up. We
stood in front of the mirror with our arms around each other. Oh my god! We
looked SO good together!
    On Friday, March 20th, I went over to Jonah's house. OH MY GOD! He looked
SO incredibly gorgeous! He was wearing jeans, a Hoodoo Gurus T-shirt and a
black paisley shirt over it. We only made out once because we were in
abnormal moods. Even though we only did that once, it was REALLY good!
    Last night Jonah and I had the BEST conversation. He said, "I'm staying
right here because I really love you." I can't tell you how flattering it is
to know how Jonah feels about me. I mean, he is this amazing person and he
has these terrific values. I believe everything Jonah says to me. Everything.

I wonder if I
have ever liked
anyone as much as
I like Zach.
He is deffinetly
different than any
others. He's cute,
funny, witty, smart, in-
timidating, cool, popular,
and has this aditude
that's almost bad. I
love it. But, I also
feel so sorry for
him. He is always
grounded. His Parents
rule his life. They
grounded him over
Winter Break because
Bitch-Lady Mrs Edwards
called his parents
and told them they
should get Zach
phyciatric help. The
nerve!
I love his
eyes. Dark brown and
mysterious. He always

listens to me and looks right into my eyes. I could melt into a puddle whenever he says my name. Some bad things about him are his aditude and Paul. Paul is part of his aditude. Paul is the most popular 7th grade snow-leapord. He's also insulting, a jerk, loud, sarcastic, and a major pain in the butt. Paul rubbed off on Zach and at times he can be an egotistical self inflamed jerk. I love him lots! No one's perfect I guess.

Editor's Note: Well of course you like Zach. He's cute with a bad attitude and needs psychiatric help. Welcome to your type!

145

I'll Take A Chance

I've lost ~~my~~ your love, and my heart is filled with pain. But I'll ~~risk~~ risk my hopeless heart for you. "It's dangerous," my mind says. "You'll risk his happiness and joy, witch I'm sorry to say is not ~~me~~ you." "I'll take a chance," I said. "I'll do whatever it takes to make ~~you~~ him mine. I'll take that chance."

Dedicated To:

I'll Take a Chance * Bree Dunscombe

I blame my parents for poems like these, written during a time when I was forbidden to listen to rap and encouraged to play Phil Collins's "Do You Remember?" on my boom box. It was dedicated to my childhood crush, my unrequited love—though I wrote equally tragic poems to Joey McIntyre.

TUCKER GREENE IS SOOOO cute!

2-22

TUCKER IS SOOO cute! Today was an awesome day. I really hope T.G likes me. He walked w/me to the buses than, he ran into me! we got on the wrong bus! HOW THRILLING

2-27

Today tucker told me that I had too much eyeshadow. What an ass! Him + Linsey were hugging. she is an ass, too!

I ♥ U Chewy!

Scott here in a totally different country. I know you don't miss me. You gave me your calling card to use to call you but if you haven't yet noticed I put it back in your wallet that same night. I hope work is well. With times and with Rich. Be careful. I don't know what I would do if something were to happen to you. I care very much about you and worry little about us. I feel as though I need your love and you don't even want mine. I grew so much when we were together. You shared so much of yourself with me and I with you. Some of my closest friends don't even know some of the things you know about me. Well let me correct myself, they do. Scott you are my closest friend. You are all I want to be with. All that we have shared I can share with no other. I'm just afraid your feelings for me will change for me while I'm here in the outback. I know we talked about it all before I left but I'm so insecure about the whole. But I can't spend all my time missing you. Because then it will seem like a year w/o you. I hope to hear from you soon.

Promise me you won't change.

tell my love forever and ever.

I ♥ U.
♥ Amy

them to our hotel.

P.S. I have our pictures next to my bed & brought them w/ me and like—

7 Everyone and No One Is Doing It

Sex

Everyone makes such a fuss about losing your virginity. Really, the best part about no longer being a virgin is just all the times you got to tell yourself, over and over again in your head, that you are no longer a virgin. The first time is never great: it hurts, it's not romantic, you are outside, there are bugs, his name is Chad . . . but you are no longer a virgin, and no one can stop you from repeating that in your head every minute of the day, well, until your thirties.

Or you could just fake it. Everyone else is.

4th street bistro   17 april 1996 6 pm

he flicks me with his
          german creamed tongue
and the beaters inside
    my hollowed stomach
whip me into a frenzy
leaving frothy mounds
    of my soul
dripping with the
thin red sauce of
.my blood
which he loves to taste,
to savor each drop
dripping from my vein
    to his
    swiss chocolate mouth.
as he bleeds me,
licks my plate clean
my knife clatters to the floor
    echoing through the kitchen
    out to the dining room
where they sit
unaware
    of the true recipe

The Beating, the Slinging, the Mixing
* Kitty Joe Sainte-Marie

Ah, the wonderful clichés of the young waitress dating the Swiss chef! This can only end badly! The affair too!

I'm the waitress.

He's the chef.

I'm nineteen.

He's thirty-seven.

The restaurant averages twenty customers a night. We had time on our hands—time to indulge in health code violations on the chopping block, and for me, bad, bad poetry that I took very seriously. Ouch! Alas, our steamy kitchen affair didn't stand the test of travel, and appropriately, I dumped him in a village in Switzerland at a table set with a bowl of his mother's Bavarian cream, perfect raspberries staring up at me.

Classy start.

Smooth finish.

the beating
the slinging
the mixing
the frying
the cooking
the sizzling

unfinished

you're like swiss —

well fed and
apathetic

Tadpole * Marc Mazique

"Tadpole" originally appeared in my zine *Satanic Toasters*, a zine I did from my late high school to early college years; *ST* was primarily filled with journal entries and surreal confessional poetry, with the random prose piece thrown in for good measure. I was seventeen years old at the time and wrote "Tadpole" to impress this really punk-rock girl I had met at a six-week precollege program in the summer of 1990. She was very into Henry Rollins, while my "influences" at the time ranged from punk and industrial music to Beat poets like Allen Ginsberg. And so I wrote this sex poem (while still very much a virgin), hoping to knock her socks off . . . let's just say things did not go as I'd expected, and leave it at that.

TADPOLE

i WISH i COULD BE THE SHEETS
yOU SWEAT AND FUCK UPON
i WISH i COULD BE THE PILLOW
yOU LAY YOU BLOWN MIND ON
i WISH i COULD BE THE MAXI-PAD
bEHIND WHICH YOU HIDE YOUR PRIZE
i WISH i COULD BE THE CONDOMS YOU HATE GUYS TO WEAR
gENTLY LICKING YOUR INSIDES
i WISH i COULD BE THE BIRTH CONTROL PILL
yOU DAILY SLIDE BETWEEN YOUR LIPS
i WISH i COULD BE THE SKINTIGHT JEANS
tHAT LONGINGLY HUG YOUR HIPS
i WISH i COULD BE THAT SWEET LOOK OF PAIN
tHAT SLOWLY INVADES YOUR FACE
i WISH i COULD BE THE INTRUDING YET WELCOME TONGUE
yOU FEEL BUT CANNOT TASTE
i WISH i COULD BE THE BOAT
tHAT GLIDES DOWN YOUR TUNNEL OF LOVE
i WISH i COULD BE THE tadpole
tHAT YOUR EGG'S SO SCARED OF
i WISH i COULD BE THE TINY DENT IN YOUR BRA
tHAT YOUR STONE HARD NIPPLE MAKES
i WISH i COULD BE THE BLOODY MESS THAT'S LEFT
wHEN YOUR HYMEN BREAKS
i WISH i COULD BE THE TICKLE IN YOUR TUMMY
yOU GET WHEN YOU COME
i WISH i COULD BE THE THROAT
tHAT YOUR TORTURED SCREAMS COME FROM
i WISH i COULD BE THE FEELING
tHAT YOU NEVER WANT TO END
i WISH i COULD BE THE ARCH
yOUR BACK QUICKLY FORMS AS IT RISES AND DESCENDS
i WISH i COULD BE THE BOY
tHAT YOUR PARENTS WARNED YOU ABOUT
i WISH i COULD BE THE INNOCENT AIR
tHAT YOU BREATHE IN AND OUT
i WISH i COULD BE THE HOT SALIVA
tHAT JUMPS BACK AND FORTH
i WISH i COULD BE THE WORD YOU'RE CHANTING
"mORE, mORE, mORE"
i WANT TO BE THE RHYTHM ECHOING OUR SONG
"mORE, mORE, mORE"

~MM
Early Sep 90

DAY Tuesday   DATE June 20, 1989
     So much has happened
since I last wrote!, Marianne
& I are friends again. We're
going to a Bon Jovi concert
the 28th! And guess what?!
Yesterday was Laura's Pool Party.
It was awesome!!! I became
friends with the popular kids.
Not good friends, but pretty friendly.

DAY   DATE
     But anyway, yesterday,
Dave asked me out!!?!
You're not gonna believe
it but I said no! It's cuz
he goes out with girls for
their looks, and dumps them
a week?! a week later. The reason he
day?! prob'ly decided to do it
then, was cuz of my bathing

DAY   DATE
     suit. It was hot pink, with
a black zipper down the front,
and the sides were open but
laced up with black material.
It was cut up to my waist,
& was pretty low-cut too.
Now, though, I wish I'd
said yes. I need a boyfriend!!

Laura's Pool Party * Lori Dalton

Was anything in life more emotionally charged than seventh grade? Bodies were changing, hormones were raging, and popularity status changed faster than we could go through our Aqua Net. On this one day, my thirteen-year-old self was thoroughly enjoying the ride. Playa asked me out because of my slutty bathing suit, and I said no.

Editor's note: I think it's safe to say that this is the only diary entry in the entire chapter that parents would be proud of. Dude asked you out because of your slutty bathing suit, and you said no. So what if you regretted it? You held your ground! YOU WIN BEING A TEENAGE GIRL! GAME OVER, DAVE!

Attention * Lori Dalton

This should be titled "Tales of a Sixth Grade Nothing." I was twelve. With mosquito bites. And a training bra. And clearly, an active imagination.

It's funny how I'm so excited about getting a bra, but not yet aware of how to use it to my advantage. It's not my *back* that's going to be getting anyone's attention.

You know, I'm getting breasts! and men usually go for that, like Justin. Rebecca doesn't have anything, but I'd say... Flat chest! Also I have L'sa and I saw it, it went great! I'm pregnant, and I'm going to school, that might give me L'sa lines...

Nice pictures! Honestly! oh well, I never did play to be an artist. Remember

June 12, 1991

What would a 45 yr.
old man with morals do?
Act apalled; at his own and
at her thoughts and actions.
Does our hero have
morals? Some; but maybe not
enough. Does our heroine have
morals? She's 15; she's tired
of morals. She's ready for
full-fledged adulthood, with
no holds barred. and it looks
like she may get exactly what
she wants.

She lies here, under the sun on
the bow of his boat. shaky
on the inside, but sultry on
the outside, at least to him.
He's about ready to either
kill himself or jump over
board. hmm... but then he
wouldn't be able to stare at
her incredibly long legs...
Her brain is telling her to
give it up and to stop rubbing

Tired of Morals * Erin Glaser

When I was fifteen, I wrote this weird third-person narrative starring my parents' friend and me. Nothing like this *ever* happened; I just had a crush on the man. But I was always worried that my mother would find it. Can you imagine if you found this, in your daughter's handwriting? It would have been pretty obvious to her who I was writing about. They would have suspected this poor clueless mature adult.

I'm thirty-two now, and for the past six years, I've been dating a man twenty-one years my senior. He's a whole person who can drink older than I am. My family cannot possibly get more weirded out than they already are.

Mingling of Souls * Danielle Henderson

I worked in a convent in high school, and it clearly had no immediate or lasting effect.

This is a classic case of taking yourself too seriously. In proper high school fashion, the object of desire was the older brother of a friend. A college man, which held endless appeal.

It will surprise no one to learn that I remained a virgin until I was twenty-two years old.

By the time I did the deed, it was such a nonevent that I didn't even know I was having sex until it was almost over. My then boyfriend tried to stop and make sure it was all right. "Um, we're definitely having sex right now." I grabbed his face gently and said, "Well, don't STOP, jeez. And please, don't ruin this for me by talking."

Since it is the most important event of my upcoming life I want to share it with him and I know (I think) men are always physically ready for sex but I want him to be emotionally ready as well. Sex is, and should be, a mingling of souls. A unification of minds. An expression of endless passion through properly fitting anatomy. If it is to be anything less I cannot share that with him, or anyone. So in essence it is a rather large step for the both of us. I need to be sure he knows how I am feeling about this, if he is indeed to be the one. When you think about it, we have only been speaking frequently for 1 month, no matter how long we've known each other. Perhaps I should slow down. And yet I cannot help but feel time is not of the matter when emotions such as these come into play.

5-29-94

Sunday night. Early Monday morning.
1:08 a.m. Memorial Day. It is hard
to write these days. I have every intention
to sit myself down with a pen & this
notebook, but it's just an intention. I'm
not inspired or moved or emotional. But
now I think I need to force something
out. Now is as good a time as any
to catch up. Work is hard. Memphis
in May finale/sunset symphony was this
past weekend. Hostessing rude people
is difficult to do with a forced smile.
good afternoon, Landry's Seafood House,
this is Heather, may I help you?
No, this is no longer Captain Bilbos,
No, we do not take reservations,
No, I do not know of any good
Restaurants on Beale. The real
world is no fun at all. Dawn is
no longer a virgin. She had the big
ess ee ex. I am still in shock
+ pain + surprise. I didn't handle
the news well & she sensed my hesitancy
She assures me that it's right, that
they're in love, that he fully respects
her, that she has no regrets. It would
be cool if I could be genuinely happy
for her, but I know what I know.
She lost her virtue & she has no idea.
I'm so sad. I'm torn between what I know
is right & what she will only-hear. I'm
not a part of her world anymore.
We shared our common virtue for so
long, as a link, + it is now severed. I
don't think things can ever be the same.
I'm not passing judgment, but our worlds
are now different. My how things change.

My How Things Change
* Heather B. Armstrong

In high school I was best friends with a girl named Dawn, and we liked to call ourselves the V Club to celebrate how we were different from all the other girls in school who were unable to preserve their virginity past the age of twelve. I was proud of my virginity in a different way than Dawn was, as I was Mormon, and virginity was my key to eternal salvation—a component in my journey toward a Mormon temple marriage, one that would result in Goddess-hood and my own planet in the afterlife. If I had sex, I would lose my planet.

Dawn just wanted to be in love when she lost her virginity, and that was good enough for me. She may not have understood my whole planet situation, but she understood that it was important to wait. This common virtue was the foundation of our friendship, and all of my memories of high school are inextricably tied to her, to the endless phone calls and hanging out after class, to the constant, burning disdain we harbored for the whores who walked among us.

After graduation she headed to Chicago, and I landed in Utah. And things were fine until the summer after our freshman year in college when she called and told me that she had had sex with her boyfriend. I acted very cool on the phone, but inside I was devastated. My best friend had become an infidel, that which we had loathed, lo, these many years. I did not care that she was in love. I could only mourn for the fact that she had come this far only to give up her shot at a planet. We would have nothing to talk about when we died.

I really did believe that I wasn't passing judgment on her decision, but that was my style: be a giant ass and call it righteousness.

Double C Cups * Joshua Newman

When I was eleven, a budding scientist at the time, a relative gave me a biography of Nikola Tesla. The biography frequently mentioned Tesla's diary, citing how central it was to his work in science. So I started keeping a diary myself. I had a Mac at the time, and, Doogie Howser–like, I kept the diary digitally. Although much of it consists of "scientific" observations, it's also scattered with personal narrative. The whole thing—including these excerpts,

related to Laura Friedman, my first love—passed from hard drive to hard drive of the many computers I've owned since, before ending up here.

June 28th, 1991
This morning I met the other CITs. One of them is named Laura. She has some Jewish last name I can't remember. Also, I think she's got double C cups. They're huge.

June 30th, 1991
Laura's pretty nice when you talk to her and she has way better teeth than Rachel. The other hot girl is named Kimmy Yewster. She lives in Queens New York the rest of the year but I guess her dad lives here in California. She's blonde but she has a New York accent and she's kind of dumb.

June 31st, 1991 [sic]
Today my group had swimming at the same time as Laura. Her last name is Friedman. Adam told me she has to have special bathing suits made because her boobs are so big.

July 4th, 1991
Josh had a barbecue at his house today. His parents are weird hippies and the whole family uses the hot tub together naked. Plus, his mom has armpit hair.

Anyway, some of the CITs were at the barbecue including Laura Friedman. We talked for a while, except neither of us said much. Sometimes talking to girls is hard work.

July 18th, 1991
Amy says I should ask out Laura because she'd say yes, except that's stupid because to go to the movies we have to ride in the back of my mom's minivan. I did that on a double date with Philip Gragg and Rachel and Laura from school. We saw If Looks Could Kill which was really good except that having to be dropped off by my mom made us look real stupid. People might have thought we were still kids instead of out on a date.

July 23rd, 1991
I kissed Laura Friedman. I KISSED LAURA FRIEDMAN. Last night was the overnight camping trip where all of the kids go to Arastradero Preserve and we make bad macaroni and cheese. We played capture the flag and I got the flag and won because I was little enough to sneak past the bigger counselors. After the campfire Laura said we should meet at 1:00 in the morning at where they park the buses and I said okay. It took forever to wait in my sleeping bag, and then I had to sneak out except it was easier than capture the flag.

Laura was waiting there and we walked to the picnic tables that are way down the hill. We couldn't use our lights because then people would see us so we kept tripping and having to grab each other to keep from falling. We were laughing when we got to the picnic table and out of breath because we were kind of running and I sat on the picnic table and Laura put her hands on my knees.

She asked if I wanted to kiss her and I said okay so we did. It was kind of weird and slippery and I don't think I was doing it right. I said I didn't think I was but Laura said I was and then we kissed again a bunch more. We snuck back to our sleeping bags and I'm supposed to see her tomorrow so I'm going to bicycle across town all the way to her house so I don't have to tell my mom to drive me. I didn't really sleep much which is good because otherwise I think I might have had a wet dream and that would be really embarrassing to clean out of a sleeping bag.

167

ride Eddie in the pole.

Palm

Cristy -n- John

steph -n- Jeff

Julie -n- Donny

Karla -n- Brad

Tammy -n- Jeff

Crissy -n- ?

Me -n- ?

chris? Eric? Doug? mark? Scott? Jerry?!!

FRIEN

DIA

HELLO KITTY
WHO KNOWS HOW MANY SECRETS ARE BURIED IN OUR DIARIES!

younger guys

MV

Nerd Grils
filth.
OUR FREE ST... NOW BUY TH...

20

happy. I haven't been this happy...
...long time.

I c... ...ened
to ... ...ta take
fore... ...er. All I know is I
hav Brooke to thank for making
my life near liveable again. Also
I am falling in very deep like
with Warren Frankford. He makes

8 No One Wants Your Gifts or Talents

The Cr
Writer

eative

Typically, the discovery that you are a writer comes right after the discovery that you own a thesaurus. The results sound like a paragraph fed through a translator three times, but man, you got to say "lain" and "cumulus" and "elixir."

Getting dumped helps too. Writing your feelings down on paper is almost as exquisite as watching yourself cry in the mirror.

Another form of inspiration is out-and-out mimicry. After you've copied the lyrics to your favorite song on the backs of your notebooks enough times, you start to feel a strange sense of personal accomplishment. *I could do this.* Of course you could. You are a teenager. You are the first person ever to have a feeling and a pen.

Dandelions

Cory and I were "intellectuals"
who frequented coffee shops, bookstores, and KMart.
Wearing large, freakish shoes,
we wandered about the city,
the black, dusty asphalt glittering beneath our feet.
We were invincible, perhaps Omniscient,
as we laughed at Summer:
fat women in halter tops,
old men in tight business suits, the pounding heat.
As his slender hands turned the pages
of volumes of poetry (Byron or Yeats),
sweat streamed down our necks.
Ignoring the stares of street preachers,
we made our way to the city cemetery,
the summer night approaching.
Our footsteps were like cats in the darkness.
Cory and I lay under a soft purple sky,
dry, scratchy weeds pressed against our backs,
bathing in the cooling winds and darkness.
We splashed barefoot in pools of stars.

Dandelions * Erin Bradley

I was probably sixteen when I wrote this. Cory was one of several boyfriends during my Goth phase. He wore a priest collar and black eyeliner and smoked so many cigarettes his front teeth were perma-stained brown at the age of seventeen.

We would walk around downtown Greenville, South Carolina (CULTURAL MECCA! A MUST SEE!), and inevitably end up making out and smoking clove cigarettes in a nearby cemetery. We called the latter "Gospel Hour with Reverend Cory" and fully believed we were the first teenagers ever to grab ass on top of a gravestone and mock organized religion.

The "large, freakish shoes" were standard-issue Doc Martens bought by our parents. Can a shoe be *freakish* if it's worn by half your high school?

"Omniscient"—This was without a doubt one of my favorite words in high school. That and *omnipotent*. I used both liberally with little to no regard for the difference in meanings. I'm still kind of unclear now. I think one means "pretentious high schooler" and the other means "*very* pretentious high schooler."

"Volumes of poetry (Byron or Yeats)"— I started reading both of these authors because they are mentioned in songs by Morrissey. Concerned parents and censors need not fear. Your teenager may slit her wrists after listening to Slipknot, but she can just as easily be influenced to read fruity British romantic poets.

"Our footsteps were like cats in the darkness"—More like cats wearing *combat boots*. What about the large, freakish shoes, Erin? Did you already forget? Are you smoking *that* much weed?

"We splashed barefoot in pools of stars"—I like how this takes a last-minute turn toward mushy Hallmark fantasy. One minute we're wearing large, freakish shoes. The next we're dipping our tootsies in puddles of astronomy. Let's hope for the sake of our ecosystem that Cory and I washed our feet.

For INSERT NAME * Joshua Neuman

This poem was originally written and given to a girl named Juanita on October 21, 1993, but was subsequently rewritten and regiven to six or seven crushes until 1995.

Maybe a good lesson to learn here is to never begin a love poem with a lumbering sad clown.

"For INSERT NAME"

I lumber like the sad clown with the hope that my performance might make you smile.
Yet I am like a flickering star over a cloudy sky.
The last time you noticed me, you launched my heart on a journey around the world and now
I'm back.
Wondering.

Is it strange that I consider you to be a long lost friend?
Or that I want to know what thoughts keep you awake at night and staring at the bedroom
ceiling?
Or whether it is your body or soul that thirsts when you rise in the morning?

Each day I see you, floating like a cloud.
I grab for the wind to figure out which one of us is moving.
INSERT NAME, is that heaven I see glowing through your skin?
Or have I misunderstood the poetry that leaves your lips every time you exhale?

To think that ink could do anything but betray your beauty
Or that this paper could ever capture the sweetness which resonates from your laughter.
But these words are my children, my only legacy in this world.
A generation raised on love.

If I were a musician, then like the Pied Piper I would play the flute in hope of awakening
the little girl within you, leading you all the way to my starving arms.
If I were a magician, I would fly you on a carpet as high as the heavens where we might
play as children and dip our bare feet in cool waters of serenity.
If I were a warrior I would chase away every demon tormenting your mind and pry apart
the dragon's suffocating grasp.
But I'm only a poet: paralyzed with pens, paper and furtive glances.

Butchered trees they cry out for help despite
The cumulus with branches they caress
Into brown bark tenderly knives they slice
For lovers briefly baringly confess
Terry loves Cody it's nineteen eighty
Two on my sixth birthday - I was smaller
Then only now I understand greatly
Strength it took the trees to faintly call her
Back for healing blood transfusion power
Dance circles round worship music I hear
Of trembling trunk that ought to tower
Cut my wrists flung muchneeded elixir
Lifeblood I lend my companions in pain
They donated leaves on which I have lain.

SONNET#ONLY BU 94

Butchered Trees * Erin Keane

I wrote a lot of painfully earnest poems as a teenager, but this one is maybe the most baffling. My writing teacher assigned a sonnet exercise based on a group nature hike, and I choked. Months later, I resurrected the idea and completed, triumphantly (or so I believed), this bizarre fantasy that apparently involves a carved-up tree receiving a human-blood transfusion. The best part? I was the least outdoorsy, wood-spritey kid in the country. I couldn't tell an elm from a birch if my life depended on it. Note the "sonnet number only" defiant sign-off—such a rebel!

Get Off the Plain! * Aaron McQuade

(a) Oftentimes, even more cringe-worthy than the horrendous material itself is the memory and knowledge of what inspired the material.

(b) I know, without any shred of doubt, that this poem is 100 percent inspired by Richard Marx.

(c) Remember that video where he moves to that town and everyone thinks he killed the mayor's (sheriff's? I forget) daughter down by the river or something? I thought that was pretty awesome.

(d) I do not, however, remember what that radish thing is about. I am very happy about this.

(e) Oatmeal still makes me giddy. Can't *explane* it.

Tara

What else could I do
I knew
The current would drag
　　　her down
What else could I say
I may
Not always be around
Where else could I turn
She learned
To listen out loud
　　　to sound
Mrs Jennings,
　I watched Your Daughter Drown.

get off the plain,
You silly fruit!

RADISH

Oatmeal makes me giddy
　like a child executioner
　　with his first guillotene
　in a blender
pour me out baby, and
　drink my pureed guts
　like it was
　　Your
　　Own:

The guts that once were mine
are now revolving in your stomach acids
Pleasantries are lost
in a tossed salad
You goddamn radish!

Why do they pass me by?
When will my Prince Charming
come and sweep me off my feet
in his Trans Am?
Maybe I'll place a want-ad

> Wanted: Male, 17 to 18 will
> accept 19, 5'8" to 6'1", fairly
> gorgeous, good sense of humor,
> Must spend time with own friends
> as I with mine.

But then, with my luck, I'd forget to
add where to apply.
                    J.W.

Trans Am Prince Charming
* Jan Arvanetes

It was the middle of Ohio, the end of the 1970s. My Bic pen felt heavy in my hand as I pulled the ink from it onto the pink three-hole-punch notebook paper. It was truly difficult, but I knew what I had to do. The words came together and perfection was found through indentation.

Later, this literary triumph found its way to page 38 of *Prism '78,* the well-known publication of poetry and fine art at Cuyahoga Falls High School. I was a mere sophomore, hopelessly struggling through the crisis that is the second year of high school. I couldn't bear to sign my full name.

Does the car really matter? Apparently, it did at the time. No woman can resist a Trans Am.

Monsieur X * Audrey Shupp Sahns

I received a series of awesomely bad love poems by mail back in 1991 when I was a shy sixteen-year-old. I had no clue who wrote them, other than the mysterious "Monsieur X." One letter was in the front door, hand-delivered with a copy of *The Watchtower,* the publication by Jehovah's Witnesses. It then dawned on me that it was the kid in my science and gym classes who was a Jehovah's Witness. So not only was he trying to woo me, but convert me as well. I finally asked him one day in gym class if it was him and he admitted it, but nothing came out of the situation, and I ended up dating someone else. I saved the poems all these years since they were so creative and he went to so much effort.

You know this guy either (a) wished he had a cape or (b) actually had a cape.

The absence of your presence makes my
heart grow fonder of you.

You walk in beauty like the night, as
your eyes are but stars that guide my
heart to your hands. Your hands are
therefore the controlers of my destiny.

You are like a Queen that comes forth
like the lonely moon from the slow
opening curtains of the clouds walking
in beauty to your midnight throne.

I ache to feel your touch as it enlight-
ens my whole.

My heart palpitates uncontrolably
when I feel you near.

You are truly an angelic force that
draws me nearer to you and makes me
advance to a borderline of awe and
insanity.

But hark, I will sit down now, but
the time will come when you shall
hear me.

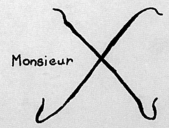

Monsieur

10/10

Natural Disaster
I cannot be the center of attention.
I cannot be out of hand.
When problems arise
things get complicated-
humid or lame.
I do not choose to "fit in".
It's a waste of time
to be laughing or smiling
all the time.
I don't worry too much-
I'm not excited to see
the great picture.
The view point of my situation
may be suprising or shocking
but to me - it's like someone is sleeping.
I don't need a group
to share my interests.
~~xxxxxxxxx~~ I cannot have bad experiences.
I cannot be the life of the party.
I don't worry about the expression on his
face,
I can have a good time
being "complicated"
or serious.
People go crazy and nuts.

Like a big earthquake.
Or a flood on the plains.
I cannot be really attractive.
I am just a natural disaster.

not true —

*It's okay to be "different" — just be who
you are.*

Natural Disaster * Millie de Chirico

This one is completely depressing on so many levels. I think the most embarrassing thing is that I actually turned this in for a grade in my English class. Can you imagine what my teacher was thinking?! Besides the fact that the whole thing reads like a really bad suicide note, it's not even well-written and kind of contradicts itself (like saying "I cannot have bad experiences" in the same breath as "it's a waste of time to be laughing or smiling all the time"). She probably felt she *had* to give me a 10 out of 10 or else I'd hang myself.

I love those scratch-out marks too, especially in the title. Hey, writers in *pain* don't use Wite-Out, man.

Obviously the most mortifying bit is what she wrote me at the end—in that Condescending Teacher Red Pen! I love how she underlined "natural disaster" at the end and wrote "not true," as if she was *changing lives* through those little notes. Of course, now the thought of a teacher telling me that "it's okay to be 'different'—just be who you are" kind of makes me want to kill myself.

Also, as a testament to how dramatic and LOOK AT ME! I was in high school, I wrote my name at the top when this assignment was supposed to be anonymous (which is why my name is crossed off in red pen in the top right-hand corner). Hey, I wanted to make sure I got credit for this epic piece of poetry!

The funny thing is, I don't even remember ever being as depressed and self-hating as this poem indicates. From the looks of this thing, I should have had a triple dose of Zoloft mainlined into my veins. This might be what happens when you listen to "Lithium" by Nirvana one too many times.

Plus, I have no idea what "humid" is supposed to mean. Really bad adjective there!

Complex * Millie de Chirico

God. I hate that there's proof that I was ever in a "defiant grunge rocker" phase.

I wrote this back in 1994, as a response to something that was said to me by the wife of my dad's best friend during Thanksgiving dinner. In fact, I think I wrote this right after I got home. During the dinner I had been receiving looks of disgust from everyone at the table. I think it was because I chose to wear a tattered red flannel shirt with black-and-white-striped tights under cutoff jean shorts to a holiday meal at my parents' friends' house. I was being dramatic and stabbing the dinner rolls with my fork for added effect, channeling Ally Sheedy from *The Breakfast Club* every chance I could.

After this grandiose display, after I basically mimed the whole "I can't be bothered with this WHITE MAN'S tradition, man!" the wife of my dad's friend finally chimed in. I remember she put her napkin down disapprovingly while shaking her head and remarked, "Oh God. Don't tell me you're turning *grunge* . . ."

Of course, when the ESTABLISHMENT finds a way to define you, it's over. That must have set me off because I marched right home and penned this masterpiece. I'm really cringing over my use of the terms "demi god" and "alterna freak," as well as my totally out-of-place Naughty by Nature reference.

Also, I like how I used the term "doing pot," as opposed to "smoking pot" or something like that. You can tell what a poseur stoner I was at that time.

I don't know why I included the line about my neighbor's parents. I don't remember any of our neighbors being huge druggies or anything. Must have been a shock tactic.

Complex

4/1"   I'm a the punk-rock

demi god, alterna freak

of the 21st century

and I can't comply,

by your finite rules

and your regulations abound.

I'm not down with that, opp

and If you think I'll

listen to you- wrong. anarchy.

I _will_ smoke with my friends

at Taco Bell. I _will_ do

pot with my neighbor's parents

in really weird places. And

you can't stop me from buying

that oversized flannel on sale

for $7.88 at Walmart-
What are you? Government?
I'll shave my head, save
the whales, be gay if I
please and still hold
the title of being the
punk-rock demi god, alterna
freak of the 21st century.

I like how I made the Wal-Mart reference, as if Wal-Mart was "alternative." Have no idea what inspired that line.

Also, I maybe shouldn't have included the "save the whales" bit. It really dates it.

By the way, this was supposed to read in the traditional 1990s coffeehouse slam style, all punchy and rage-fueled, which is why I wrote, "Wrong. Anarchy." Terrible.

Captain E * Aaron McQuade

My plan for this song was exceptionally well thought-out. I needed to tell Erika how I felt about her. But I needed to do so without actually telling her how I felt about her. So I decided to write a song to her, but to do it in a way that made my subject somewhat ambiguous. Step two was to record the song. I then needed to find a mutual friend who would be perceptive enough to figure out that the song was about her, and caring enough to give her a copy of the song so that she could be blown away by my master wordsmithing; the deep, deep emotion behind it; and my amazing performance.

I never got to step two.

Here I am calling you one final time
I finally found the mountain that I couldn't climb

This is great for two reasons. First, it implies that before now I had seen nothing but success with love. Second, there's my brilliant double entendre. See, Erika was extraordinarily well-endowed. Get it? Mountains?

The children are all falling at my feet
But there's no way out of this one, Captain E

Regarding the "children falling at my feet" line, I have no idea what it means, but I know I really liked the way it sounded—because I've found it

Captain E

Here I am calling you one final time
I finally found the mountain that I
couldn't climb

The children are all falling at my feet
But there's no way out of this one, Captain E

I can't do anything but stare at the sky
You took my heart and shot it like a ham on Rye

I wish ~~for~~ for someone else that I could be
No way...

I've known you for so long
But you don't know just who I am
I know you'd think it's wrong
But I wish I could tell you what's in my head

Your Mountains will never crumble to my sea
And there's no way out of this one, Capt E

Captain E, cont.

used in five or six other songs. I'll leave this for my therapist to figure out. On my decision to refer to Erika as "Captain E," this was in case our mutual friend wasn't perceptive enough. In hindsight, I realize now that someone hearing this song could have come to two conclusions: One, "Oh my God, Aaron's in love with Erika," or two, "Oh my God, Aaron's on ecstasy."

> *I can't do anything but stare at the sky*
> *You took my heart and ate it like a ham on rye*

See? Master wordsmithing.

> *I wish for someone else that I could be*
> *But there's no way out of this one, Captain E*
> *I've known you for so long*
> *But you don't know just who I am*
> *I know you'd think it's wrong*
> *But I wish I could tell you what's in my hand*

I have never met a woman in my life who would have heard these lines and not been immediately and powerfully repulsed.

> *Your mountains will never crumble to my sea*

(Sigh)

> *And there's no way out of this one, Captain E*

> Devil: Hello there Juan welcome to my home
> Don't get to comfortable with the fire and brimstone
> MAN: My name's not Juan, sir tell me why do you keep calling me that

The Devil and Not Juan * Aaron McQuade

I was sixteen, and I had just seen The Who's *Tommy*, and I thought, "Well, I could do better than *that*." Only I abandoned my rock opera after three lines. We never even learned Not Juan's real name.

193

(3) "Kid Gloves"   - Rush
"The Weapon"   - RUSH
(9) "Twilight Zone" - RUSH
(10) "Good Day in Hell"   - Eagles
(2) "Already Gone"   - Eagles
"Desperado"   - Eagles
"Superman"   - The Kinks ✓
"All Day and All of the Night" - The Kinks
"Stairway to Heaven" - Led Zeppelin
"A Rock and a Hard Place" - The Sisters of Mercy
"~~Never~~ Never Enough" - The Cure
"The Whole Truth" - Wartime
(8) "White Room" - Cream
"Joy to the World" - Three Dog Night ✓
"Shook me all Night Long" - AC/DC ✓
(6) "And She Was" - Talking Heads
(1) "Magic Carpet Ride" - Steppenwolf
"Empty Spaces" - Roger Waters

Mix Tape * Josh Gallaway

This list neatly provokes all at once all the emotions this book gives me. Inclusion of three Rush songs makes me cringe, and three Eagles songs makes me cringe. But the Sisters are there, as are the Cure, and I'm proud of fourteen-year-old Josh when I see that. He's cool, and this is the taste I have as an adult. And Wartime—that trumps the musical taste of any person you can find in current-day Brooklyn. Josh will be a music snob, we can clearly see. But everything of my adult self is there: it's awkward, and there are a lot of parts that seem out of place—like a bunch of Eagles songs next to Henry Rollins—but this is because you're trying out different things when you're young, borrowing personality and taste from other people in a clumsy, obvious way.

And please note: I crossed out "Stairway to Heaven." If I hadn't had that minimum amount of sense, I might have been doomed, my teenage years might have eaten me. Thank god I didn't make anyone a mix tape with a prom theme on it. Gabba gabba hey.

ED VED * Elizabeth Goodman

This elegy to the lost love of my fifteen-year-old life, Eddie Vedder, lives in a hideous fabric-covered notebook I keep under my bed with all the others. A decade of treatises written against boys whose names I can't remember. Entire spiral-bound notebooks filled with pressed flowers from some mushroom-fueled camping trip in northern New Mexico taken the summer I got my Volvo (my parents were hippies, obviously). And throngs of essays in which I profess my love for Gavin Rossdale. What I'm saying is, you're lucky you're getting Eddie (or ED VED, as I refer to him in the ugly journal). You could be reading about why Gavin is God.

When I was fifteen, Pearl Jam inspired me to merge my thing for popular music with my overintellectualized type A schoolgirl's need to do book reports on everything that mattered to me. In my special Pearl Jam notebook, I collected carefully self-annotated copies of every article ever written about the band, most of which I'd printed out from microfiche at my school's library. When I wrote about Eddie, I only used my sacred purple Pilot Precise pens because they were purple, and precise, and my favorite, and I felt like he could very possibly see what I was writing about him and would be offended if I used, like, green. Now that I'm paid to write like a fan girl, I use any pen I can find. I don't love Pearl Jam the way I used to, and I don't listen to their early records with any regularity. But in 1996 my entire life was a book report on Pearl Jam. And I totally got an A.

Eddie once said "I'm still that fucking surfer gas station guy who plays music. So I write fans back a normal letter and find myself becoming part of their lives, a part they need, and they keep needing more & more."

As much as I would like to say I wasn't. I am. I am one of those fans who needs him. We all need him w/out really knowing him. But he is a part of their lives before he writes back to them. He is that part as soon as he writes those songs he wishes he didn't have to write. The ones that mean something essential & untouched to him. We can feel that. Wait, I don't really know why it is that I feel the way I do about this music so I cannot pretend to know why other feel that way. I guess that music & my thoughts are

Heather Ellis
November 6th
3rd Period
Choice Poem # 10

EDDIE

SINGING UP ON STAGE
YOUR EYES DANCING WITH RAGE
USING MUSIC AS A BRIDGE
TO REACH UNKNOWING KIDS
THEY THINK IT'S JUST A GAME
AND IT DRIVES YOU INSANE
TO THINK THEY DON'T UNDERSTAND
YET YOU COME FROM COMMON LAND
EVERYTHING WHICH IS SACRED TO YOU
DOESN'T HELP THEM FIND A CLUE
YOU'VE MISSED ANOTHER TARGET
WITH A MESSAGE YOU CAN'T FORGET
IT IS SOMETHING THEY CAN'T PERCEIVE
AND A TRUTH THEY WON'T RECEIVE
NOW YOU WISH YOU NEVER SHARED
BECAUSE IN RETURN YOU GET A BLANK STARE

RECITING YOUR LYRICS FULL OF HATE
THE POINTS YOU'RE TRYING TO STATE
DO NOT COME ACROSS
AND ANOTHER AUDIENCE IS LOST

EDDIE * Heather Burford

You couldn't grow up in the Seattle suburbs in the 1990s without Eddie impacting your life. And apparently I sooo got him. I wrote this poem after seeing Pearl Jam in concert with my dad. WITH MY DAD.

I like to picture Eddie Vedder leaving the stage, wiping sweat from his brow, opening his bottled water—distracted and distraught that yet another audience lost his message.

Actually, that probably happened a lot.

Editor's note: I really expected more Kurt Cobain poems, but it seems the formula to inspiring teenage girls in the 1990s was not killing yourself and battling Ticketmaster.

change
you
ve cris
uld the drinkin
e be lowered?
ye
older
guys
wild

yesterday. He is still beautiful
but he was rude and sarcastic.
What an asshole. He really made
me mad. I want to inflict great
pain and suffering on him. He made
me so mad. I got the shakes I was

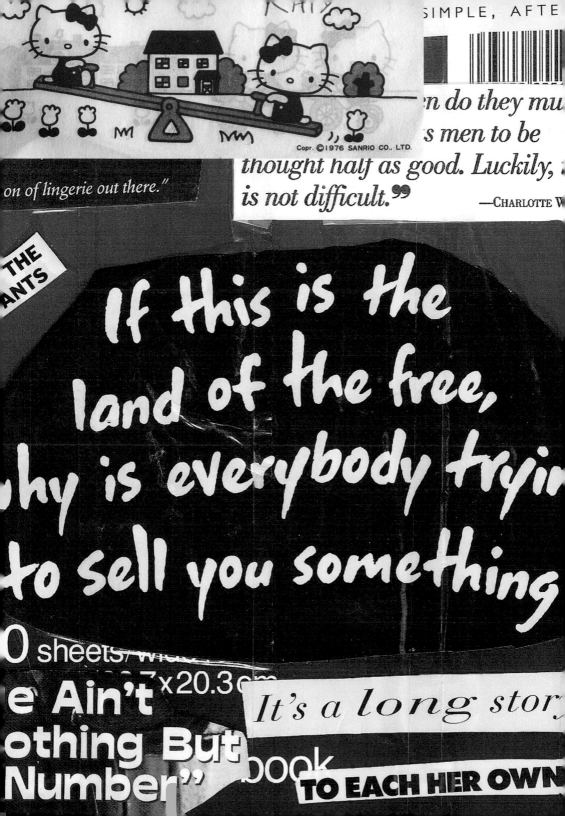

9 Teenage Fan Club

Letters Famous

to
People

The fan letter is a delicate balance. You can't help but gush, but you don't want to come across as just a fan. Even though you are. You're not like the other fans, though. You are different. You and this unknown famous person, you two could have a real bond. You could be peers. You could share inside jokes. You have to word everything just right, so your coolness comes across immediately, and they realize the relationship they're missing out on, not knowing you, sweaty teenage you, writing in your spiral notebook at your parents' kitchen table in Ohio.

Selecting the right ink color is *crucial.*

9 Derby Dr.
Fredericksburg, VA 22405
29 August 1991

Dear Ladies and Gentlemen,

Over the past few months I have become a regular follower of your show, "Beverly Hills, 90210." I have seen many positive aspects in each of the shows. It is interesting to see a teen show addressing current topics and trying to deal with them in a responsible manner. I'm glad that shows like yours exist.

As always, there is room for change. Before I get to that, let me first tell you about myself so that you can understand my perspective. I will be a senior in high school this year. I don't hang out with the popular crowd, but at my school there are no fine lines between cliques. I talk with all kinds of people and consider many varied and interesting people to be my friends, no matter what their social standing. I'm usually with the more intelligent crowd because their behavior usually tends to be good and they tend to grasp ordinary situations and conversations pretty well. At least most of the time they do.

I like all the characters on "Beverly Hills 90210." I think that "the death of Brandon Walsh" would be a great topic for you to cover. I like the guy and everything, but he's just too great a character. He holds the whole group together. Without him the unity amongst all these friends would be lost. For a few episodes chaos would reign. In those episodes you could experiment with different types of story telling. Make the show more like "Twin Peaks," but geared for a younger generation. "Twin Peaks" was followed by a lot of teens, but I don't think it was advertised to that age group. It would be neat to see this type of visual reality twisting on show which claims to be strongly routed in reality. It would be fun for the writing staff and allow them the opportunity to clear the minds and have fun with the show before the third season gets underway. "The death of Brandon Walsh" would be a good transition for new students who need to be focused on. I'm quite upset that these students will be remaining in the eleventh grade. It's bad enough that the actors probably aren't under twenty. Bring in more new faces and allow the current cast to experiment with different projects. Quarterly reunions would be fun. And occasionally, on the show, follow the kids in their post high school lives.

I hope you think about some of the suggestions I've made. Always remember to keep things in constant motion. Make sure the video camera guy uses his camera right, he's always pointing it at the backs of people's heads. And what does he do with all those tapes?

That's all for now,

Marc (just another face in the crowd) Balgavy

NOT

SNL is Paisley Chair!

The Death of Brandon Walsh
* Marc Balgavy

The teenage Marc Balgavy spent a lot of time searching through *TV Guide*, highlighting which programs he was going to watch during the upcoming week. In high school I started a video club and always made sure to get the best TV for class presentations. In short, I was a bit of an AV nerd. I did have good friends, and, as my letter shows, I was totally unfamiliar with the hierarchy of high school life.

During the age before widespread use of the Internet, I would search *TV Guide* to find addresses of broadcasters. Fueled by writing campaigns to save favorite shows and an unhealthy obsession with the letters page in Marvel Comics, I would occasionally trot out the typewriter and send ridiculous notes to the creators of favorite TV programs.

In looking at this letter now I can't tell if I'm impressed with how serious, yet obviously nonserious, I was, or if I'm a little scared and put off by that tone. My letter was addressed to the Writing Staff of *Beverly Hills, 90210,* c/o the Fox Broadcasting Company. I'm pretty sure I secretly dreamed they would write back with a job offer. I was saddened, upset, and forced to write another letter when the only response I received was a full-color flyer promoting 90210 merchandise.

Miss S. Gilbert, USA * Holly Burns

This is a fan letter I wrote (and thankfully never mailed) to Sara Gilbert, who played Darlene on *Roseanne,* and with whom I was slightly obsessed. I wrote from boarding school, asking relationship advice. It goes on and on. I've included the envelope as well, with its three sweetly hopeful airmail stickers. Please note that I didn't even bother with a city or state, so certain was I that "Miss S. Gilbert, 10000 Santa Monica Boulevard, USA" would be enough to get it to her.

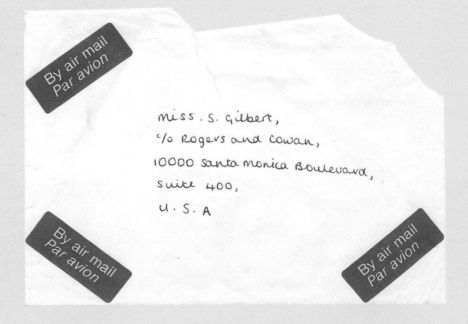

miss. S. Gilbert,
c/o Rogers and Cowan,
10000 Santa Monica Boulevard,
Suite 400,
U.S.A

Tully's Head House,
Farnham Lane,
Haslemere, Surrey
GU27 IHD
ENGLAND.

Dear Sara,

This is probably strange getting fan mail from a girl, but I just wanted to say 'hi' and now I think you're really great on the show. I can't believe you work with Johnny Galecki! what's he like? Seriously, I am so addicted to your show, cos I live in England the TV isn't that great, and 'Roseanne' is the best programme I've watched ever! I can't believe you guys (well Darlene and David) split up on the show. Sorry, I know I'm talking as if you really ARE Darlene in real life, but it really feels like it, it feels like I know you as a friend. You see, I'm having some problems right now with a friend and a guy, and it feels like you are sort of a role model, someone I can talk to and relate to. Sorry, I'm talking crap - I'm sorry if I'm boring you to death - I just need to talk to someone and you're so much like me on the show and......
I'm sorry, I know people aren't their characters on TV but you just seem so great and perfect and funny and I feel like I know you - like you're a big sister or something. I'm not screwed up, really, although this letter does imply that I am. Put it down if you want, it's a load of crap - I need a friend.
Look, Sara, I'm really sorry for writing all this crap to you, I just needed to talk, and I feel like I know you (or Darlene should I say) like a friend; no, better than one of my friends. I'm really sorry if I've wasted your time. I hope you don't think I'm screwed up.
                    Love,
              Holly xxx

Dear David & Gillian,

Hi! My name is Tracie ~~Masek~~.
I'm in seventh grade and I live in Westerville
Ohio. It's kind of boring here, ~~~~

~~~~
~~~~

I love
sports
of any
kind but
my
favorite
is soccer.
I play on
~~~~ a team
called
the
Sharks.
We're
pretty
pathetic.
So What
are you're
favorite
sports?

▶ I was wonder if you could please
send me an autographed of you.
I watch The X-Files every time
it's on. It is my favorite show.
You are both very good actors.
Keep up the good work.

                    Your ~~friend~~,
                         Tracie Másek
                    friend

P.S. My address is:

[REDACTED]

Write back soon!

X-Files
Zachery Ty Bryan
~~Dean Cain~~
Eddie Furlong
? Leonardo DiCaprio ?
? Macaulay Culkin ?
Ethan Hawke
Andrew Keegan
? ~~~~ ?
~~Keanu Reeves~~

Rider Strong
Justin Whalin
Jonathan Taylor Thomas

Your Friend * Tracie Masek

This is a draft of a letter that I wrote to David Duchovny and Gillian Anderson, requesting their autographs. It was also used as a template for other celebrities, which explains the list of celebrities found near the bottom. Apparently I thought I was too good for the youngest son from *Home Improvement*.

The decision to go with "friend" instead of "#1 fan" was the right one.

Dear Doogie * Johanna Gohmann

I was thirteen when the amazing boy doctor, Doogie Howser, M.D., captured the hearts of my middle-school friends. My girlfriends went on and on about this Doogie person, but I never tuned in to the show, as I was in the process of shifting my obsessive girlhood crushes away from television and toward the stars of the silver screen. I also think I was a bit turned off by the name "Doogie." But one night at a friend's urging, I finally caught an episode and, of course, was immediately smitten. Neil Patrick Harris was everything a small-town girl on the cusp of puberty could want: cherub-faced, devoid of body hair, and gay. I fell pretty hard, and not only penned a fan letter, I actually mailed it. I know for a fact that I mailed it, because six years later, a forwarded postcard from the Neil Patrick Harris Fan Club turned up in my college mailbox. It featured a glossy photo of Neil, and a short message updating me on his current career plans. Naturally, my college friends assumed someone had signed me up for the club as a joke. They all had a good laugh, and I chuckled right along with them, pretending to wonder who on earth would *do* such a thing.

Dear Neil,

I have never written to a celebrity before, but I figure it's no different than writing to a friend. Besides the fact that they aren't teen idols and don't recieve fan mail, what's the difference, right?

Now, I'm not writing because I want your underwear, or a lock of your hair, or anything goofy like that. I just wanted to tell you that I respect you a lot both as an actor and a person. I act a lot myself, and I enjoy watching how you interpret your Boogie character every week. I have seen you on various talk shows and have read a couple articles, and it seems to me that you are one funny, classy guy.

But I must admit, the first time I watched your show I only did so because my friend kept telling

me how good it was, and I read
somewhere that you and I share one of the
same favorite actors, John Lithgow,
so I figured, anybody that likes
John Lithgow, (There isn't an over
abundance of people that do) can't
be all that bad. So I watched, and I
was very impressed, your Doogie is
a very believable one, and now your
show has become one of the few
shows I watch "sorta" every week (I'm more
of a movie fan, myself.)
     Well, I know what with
your series + fan mail, you haven't got
a lot of time for small time actresses
like myself, but if your mother or secretary
or whoever, helps with your fanmail, if you
could manage t, I'd love an autographed
picture! Congradulations on your success, and
I wish you luck in the future. Sincerely yours,
  P.S.- Tell Dobby bottle she's one lucky   Su Bohman
              gal!   Address

Isn't it great? Why am I in such a great mood? (?) I've got no idea. But it's awesome! I haven't been in one for a super long time! (ya know?) Now that it's getting close to Summer, I wonder who I'm gonna meet? I mean seriously meet.

Mon.	Tues.	Wed.	Thus.
3:00	~~6~~		
2:00	~~8~~ ~~14~~	~~15~~	~~16~~ ~~23~~
12:30	~~21~~	12:00 ~~30~~	
	2:30 ~~6~~	12:30 ~~7~~	
	11:00 ~~13~~	11:00 **14**	

PICTURE PERFECT!

August 22nd

~~Dear,~~

ar Diary,

The Rick Springfield concert was a blast. I love Rick Springfield now. he shook my han It was his Bithday t someone brougnt a cake he ate it. And he acted like it was food poisonin He is so very Georgeous. I have to

Last Will &
Testame

ls and
nts

Whether prompted by fear or curiosity, every teenager writes a will and has a death fantasy. So that you can envision how much your parents will regret ever having punished you. So that you can imagine your secret crush being crushed by the news of your death. "Oh, if only I'd known!" they'd wail, gnashing their teeth and beating their breast. "I never would have grounded her on the night of the INXS concert!" "I would have revealed my true feelings before her untimely demise!"

Of course, there was the practical side too. In light of an unfortunate accident that could leave you sprawled dramatically on your deathbed, *someone* needed to think about where your Luke Perry posters would end up.

Will expires: 1993

I, Elizabeth Coen being of sound mind and body hearby proclaim the following items to the following people:

Briana: This Book, and the one written before it (in my toy box), my ←Big one Luke Perry Poster & Jason Priestley Poster, & my Leonardo Decaprio one too (if she wants it!) in desk drawers w/ other pictures blackmail pictures

Heather: my trolls & my gnarlies, my caboodles w/ all my make up in it.

Amber: my stereo

Alysen (Allson, Allison, Alicen, Allyson, Alg Fronuse????) ha ha →

next page

Expires 1993 * Liz Kellermeyer

I wrote this shortly after a close friend of mine, Alexis, died in seventh grade. It was the first time death felt very real to me, and it scared me. I remember wishing that I had something of hers to remember her by, wishing that she had been able to leave some sort of good-bye for the rest of us. I'm sure those feelings inspired my desire to do what Alexis had not been able to and give my most precious items to the most precious people in my life.

However, being thirteen years old, my generous benefaction ranged from a Luke Perry poster (the big one) to the return of a friend's toothbrush she'd apparently left at my house. I'm sure I imagined my death would be tragic in some way and my friends would clutch dearly to their Boyz II Men tapes, cat pictures, and bags of shredded money (from the gift shop in the Mint) and be glad they had some little token by which to remember my spirit.

I guess my parents would have had to make do with whatever was left over.

her toothbrush & toothpaste
(on my shelf), my
watermelon earrings &
anything eles she wants
on my jewlery hanger,

Yasmeen: All my notes (on
my shelf in a
tin near the grey
bear

Summer: my cat picture
above my bed
(Heather gave it to
me and I'm sure
Summer will take
as good care of it
as I did)

Jonathan: my shredded money,
Winter (my teddy
bear), the little
things and their
homes (above my
bulliten board)

Tel: Note that Follows

Nakia: Tapes: Boyz II
       Men, BBD, Minah
       Cary, Fresh Prince,
       Amy Grante, etc.

PS
⌐ want to
be cremated
And put next
to Lexis,

Don't Let This Bring You Down
* Liz Kellermeyer

I find it hilarious that my note to Tel—a friend, sure, but moreover, a notorious big mouth—is ostensibly a way to let Nathan S. know I had the hots for him.

Dear Tel,
        Hi, well I guess
this is my final
goodbye to you. look,
    I know I got
on your nerves some
times but I'm really
sorry for all the
times we didn't get
along. I don't know
if you knew this,
    but you were my
best guy friend - so
thanx for listening
to me these last
few years. Don't let
this bring you down.
I'm happy now. I'M
sure I'm with Alexis
    Hey, did you know I
had a big crush on
Nathan S. for a while?
Tell him. I'll miss him
and you, and everyone.

                I love you guys
Love,
Elizabeth coen

May 21, 1994

ERINN'S WILL

Since I'm having surgery on Tuesday I'm writing a will. I know this surgery is only on my knee, but I'd like to take some precautions. Mom and Dad, since you're the people who'll probably read this first, please give the letters following this will to the proper people. Anyway, there are some things I'd like to give to people. Please give the money in my bank accound (305$), and any other cash in my room to the ADA ~~reseach~~ research. Let Brian have any of my clothes he wants and then give the rest to my friends, so they can have something to remember me by. Please give all my Midicha stuff to Kathy Korol. Mom and Dad, please read all of my diaries and then keep them to show Brian's daughters. There will be some stuff in my diaries that you won't approve of, but I want you to know about everything that happened in my life. Anyway, this is the end of my will. I just ~~realized~~ realized, you'll have to copy the letters I'm writing on the following pages because I'll be saving trees and writing on 2 sides of paper. Love-Erinn ♡

P.S. Please give all my trolls to the Zacharski girls.

Saving Trees * Erinn Foley

When I was sixteen, I had knee surgery. I wrote out wills to everyone I knew because I was certain I was going to die. The letters are hysterical, especially since at the time I was certain that I was a Christian and saving myself for marriage (I lost my virginity two months later), and I wrote letters to people who were not Christian, begging them to go to church. Nowadays I cringe every time I read that crap. I am such the agnostic liberal.

I think making sure that my trolls went to the Zacharski girls was an especially nice touch. One never knows what to do with the troll dolls in a situation like this.

I Always Loved Attention
* Ariel Meadow Stallings

As a teenager, you don't have to be suicidal (or even Goth) to ponder the great unknown of what would happen to the world if you died. Really, all you need to be is a narcissist and, as my last will and testament proves, I was clearly one of those. My favorite part of the will is the faux blasé existentialist pondering about death just being a "new experience." I also like the reference to alerting my pen pals that I'd died. For god's sake, won't somebody think of the pen friends?!

My Last Will & Testament
October 14, 1990

So, I'm dead. Well, new experiences every day. Huh. I hope that all
of you (referring to all I love and care for) are not too miserable
or anything. Remember, take time to greive and then move on, okay?

All my stuff goes to Mom, Dad, Susannah, Katherine, Tia & Suz. I do
not want to be cremated. Return me to the earth as I am, not as
black, polluting soot. Besides, I hate the thought of burning.

I will miss you all desperately. Please make sure that people I cor-
respond with through the mail know that I've "moved on to a higher
plane of being." Please have a memorial for me at school   is that
asking too much.

You have permission to read my diaries, publish any of my writings,
etc. Ha. I flatter myself.

Katherine: chill out. Don't be so miserable.

That's all. Please don't forget me. I always loved attention.

I love you all,
Ariel Meadow Stallings

Hello World!
   This is my declaration
from a young and in-
nocent child to a big,
bad, delightful, fascin-
ating, boring, shocking
world. Now there is
something out there,
called LOVE, I want it,
I want a real relations

I really LOVE Baby-sitters
Club books!

DAWN MALLORY CLAUDIA
JESSI KRISTY STACEY
MARY ANNE

SCRATCH AND SMELL
Jelly Beans

Well, I have to go finish my book report on Anne Frank. I wonder if this journal will ever make it that big!!!

Mbriah

just one week

one by one
the lonely days
slip slowly by
in a dreary haze
the sun comes up
the sun goes down
silence falls
upon the town
a day gone by
and what to show?
nothing to say
nothing to know
nothing to do
nothing to care
go to school
just sit there
back on home
uncaring eyes
the mother waits

to fuss, to fuss
do your work
hook + eyes
red or navy belt
go to bed
wake up now
wish you were dead
wish you were dead

just one week

one by one
the happy days
ecstatic dawn
dreamy haze
smile at everyone
short or tall
laugh with creatures
great and small
do your work
make them proud

Harry Connick, Jr

BROKE
BROKE

DO I
DO I ♡ YA BABY
YEAH YEAH YEAH YEA
MORE THAN EVE

Sarah
11-9-91

I CAN'T FUCKING DO IT
TO MANY GODDAMN ASSHOLES
LIVE IN MY FUCKING FACE
SPEND THERE TIME PISSIN
ME OFF.

Afterthought

If there's one thing that this experience has taught me, it's that I have zero patience for teenagers. When I was a teenager myself, I always thought I'd be one of those cool adults who Understood and Listened, but now I realize that my reaction to any current angst is *Please, go form your personality somewhere far away from me.* Yes, life is hard, but you are not the first person to ever have a thought, and right now your skin is so supple. Go draw on your notebook. Wait it out. It doesn't seem like the end will come, but it will, and then your reward will be all the easy laughs you'll get at your own past expense. It is almost worth it.

I mean, look at all these people, at one time insufferable adolescents themselves, but now they've grown up and become actual cool adults, able to look back at this painful, embarrassing time in their lives with a sense of humor. Many of these contributors are now successful writers, artists, and musicians, crafting creatively about their thoughts and feelings for a living. Only one or two ended up in prison. I won't say which ones, but go back and read through it again and let me know your guesses. The point is, they all made it out alive. That's all you can hope for from adolescence: survival. Maybe some tongue kissing. But just living to tell the tale, preferably to a bar full of your peers, is pretty impressive.

I don't really think of *Cringe* as selling out my teenage self. In all honesty, my teenage self would have been thrilled to death to think that my writing would be published one day, although probably wouldn't have been as pleased with the accompanying mocking commentary. Every diarist harbors a secret Anne Frank complex; you want your struggle to be that important. But it's not; you're hairy and awkward and there is nothing noble about your plight. Lucky for you.

Acknowledgments

There are many people without whom this book would not exist. I'd like to thank:

Donald O'Finn and Matt Kuhn at Freddy's Bar and Backroom in Brooklyn for the space and all the free drinks;

Steve Baker at ABC *Nightline* for launching the blitzkrieg press coverage that resulted in this book;

My agent and friend Anne Garrett at the James Fitzgerald Agency, for the patience, guidance, and advice;

Jim Fitzgerald, for all the connections, Oklahoma and New York;

Brandi Bowles, Erin LaCour, Min Lee, Jay Sones, and everyone at Crown for all their help; especially my editor, Carrie Thornton, for sharing my sense of humor;

Jay Carlson and Aaron Dallas for the technical skills and site-building;

Quinn Heraty and Kaiser Wahab for the legal counsel and explanations;

John Lewis and Heather Armstrong for the online support and encouragement since 2001;

Megan Berk; Dale, Pam, and Stephen Brown; Tiffany Broyles, Ryan Chittum, David and Marellie Littlefield; Emily and Tony Lytle; Sarah Niersbach; Laura Sullivan; and Joey Zielazinski for everything;

Michael Mason for being the conduit, and David Snedden for being Himself.

More than anything, I'd like to thank all the contibutors and everyone who has ever read at Cringe for selling out their teenage selves for a laugh.

You don't notice me
because I am silent.
I stand on the outside,
out of the the way
and out sight.

I know everything about you,
but you don't even know
my name.

YER OUT!

RACISM. STOP IT!
March 21 1997

off center

(contain)!
armé, je peu

Sky's the LIMIT!

05 october 1996 saturday
i don't even have any
to say, except that im dying. t
is   why i have abandonn
you. but after my death,
i   wonder. what happene
will i forget if i don't
       w i saw the face of
         approaching me, hic
         masks of all so
         never bluffing me?
         its precense withou
                i feel it w
                nto my heart
         lering wound, Th
         sore left to infe
me   and kill me slow
by   writing this, by tell
your this i am admitt

ah yes, my childhood n
more life is my nightma
now, i need to fantasizes
and when i reach for
comfort in the night—

Contributor Bios

Heather B. Armstrong is a recovering Mormon and award-winning blogger. Despite living in Salt Lake City, Utah, she maintains a healthy relationship with those who consume small children inside the Mormon temple. She is married and keeps her husband on a short leash. Along with her daughter and dog. They all pee on paper as of this writing. She can be found on her popular site, dooce, at www.dooce.com and periodically appearing on Alpha Mom www.alphamom.com/dooce/ where she writes about popular culture.

Jan Arvanetes grew up in Ohio but is now doing time in Texas as a design strategist for an IT consulting firm. Her sculptor husband, Andrew, does not own a Trans Am. And never will.

Marc Balgavy lives in Brooklyn, New York. He swears he wanted sideburns before he saw them on Dylan McKay and Brandon Walsh.

Jen Bandini is a visual artist and writer living in New York City with a large dog, a crooked cat, and a more than understanding man. Her chronicles and existential musings have found a public home at escapetonewyork.net.

Jennifer Boyer is now an editor for an international animal advocacy organization. She still, on occasion, lets her angst and woe splash onto the pages of her beleaguered journal.

Alice Bradley is the author of the blog Finslippy. Hailed as "the greatest of the mommy blogs" by the National Review Online, Finslippy has also been featured in *Redbook*, the *Oakland Tribune*, the *Newark Star-Ledger*, and the *New York Times*. Alice writes a weekly column on current events for AlphaMom, and has contributed to the *Onion* and PBS.org. She has appeared as a pop-culture commentator on the Bravo network, and as an Alpha Mom on *Good Morning America*. She has an MFA in writing from the New School University, and her fiction has appeared in several literary journals. Alice lives with her family in New Jersey.

Erin Bradley is the author of Miss Information, a weekly sex-and-dating advice column appearing on Nerve.com. She lives in the East Village in New York City and is a grateful recovering Goth.

Heather Burford lives in Spokane, Washington, where she is a marketing coordinator for an IP law firm. She and her sister saw Pearl Jam together again in 2006. Their dad didn't chaperone this time around and, thankfully, another poem was not penned.

Holly Burns is a British writer who lives in San Francisco and updates when she remembers at www.nothingbutbonfires.com. She often wonders whether Sara Gilbert would have written back. She likes to think she would have.

Brian Byrne eventually made out with a girl. He lives in Chicago with his wife and their son, Henry. Despite the city's intensely cold winters, Mr. Byrne reports a 20 to 30 percent decrease in soul-torture. He would like to thank the good people at Eli Lilly for their pioneering work in developing modern antidepressant technology.

Jay Carlson produces The Plug (www.ThePlug.net), an online magazine and series of books dedicated to creative life documentation. In his spare time, he is a famous lawyer and astronaut and makes a million dollars.

Tracy Carr grew up in Garland, Texas, where instead of actually speaking to the boys she had crushes on, she would carefully document what they ate for lunch and then analyze her findings for nutritional content and/or deep meaning. She is now a librarian in Jackson, Mississippi.

Lori Dalton lives in Los Angeles, where she continues writing a journal online under the moniker Lori MacBlogger.

Millie de Chirico is a classic movie television programmer and freelance writer living in Atlanta, Georgia. She is no longer grunge (she thinks).

Bree Ma'Ayteh Dunscombe is now happily married and no longer pines for her childhood crush. You can read more of her bad poetry at What're You Lookin' At? www.LookingAtFrema.com.

Gabrielle Fine is a photographer, illustrator, and graphic novelist who lives in Seattle, Washington. She still occasionally takes bubble baths, makes mix tapes, and tells herself how cute she is.

Erinn Foley is a recreation therapist living in the Detroit area. She still enjoys journal writing. None of the relationships mentioned turned into anything but a headache.

Josh Gallaway grew up in a small town on the Tennessee River. Currently he is a scientist and lives in New York City. Find him at Freddy's Bar and Backroom, home of the Cringe reading series.

Erin Glaser lives and works in Tempe, Arizona with her ridiculously patient boyfriend. You can find her online at www.OutOfCharacter.net.

Johanna Gohmann is a writer living in Brooklyn, New York. You can currently catch Neil Patrick Harris starring in *How I Met Your Mother* on CBS.

And you can catch Johanna blushing and changing the channel whenever she sees an ad for it.

Elizabeth Goodman grew up in Corrales, New Mexico. Since moving to New York City in 2002, her writing has appeared in *Spin*, the *NME*, *Elle*, *Nylon*, and *Rolling Stone*. She is now an editor at large at *Blender* magazine and author of the upcoming book *Cat Power: A Good Woman*. She lives with her boyfriend and two basset hounds, Jerry Orbach and Joni Mitchell.

Dana A. Gulino lives in New Jersey with her husband, three pets, and a kid on the way. She is a project manager for a company that installs solar panels, and she hopes that contributing to this book somehow enables her to retire at the ripe old age of thirty-one. Keep your fingers crossed.

Sandra Heikkinen, who hasn't planned anything so thoroughly since writing this composition, lives and works in New York City.

Danielle Henderson likes to sit on the toilet reading books until her legs go numb. She spent many ill-advised years in Alaska, where she mingled souls exclusively with Jameson whiskey. She's taller than you think and older than she looks.

Greg Howard works as a marketing director in northern California. Aside from the selection in this book and his personal website, www.GeeseAplenty.com, his major writing projects consist of several shopping lists and a sestina about yaks.

Maggie Jacobstein has always had an interest in recording the tales of her own life, as well as the lives of others. Originally from Rochester, New York, and now oscillating between Brooklyn, New York, and Cambridge,

Massachusetts, Maggie is working toward her master of arts degree in education.

Erin Keane doesn't really know (or care) much about trees. She is the author of *The Gravity Soundtrack*, a collection of poems published in October 2007 by WordFarm, and lives in Louisville, Kentucky, where she directs the InKY Reading Series and teaches Pop Music in American Literature at Bellarmine University.

Blaise Kearsley lives in Brooklyn, New York. She's funny and cute and totally over Mark, Wade, AND Jonah. She proves it fairly regularly at www.bazima.com.

Liz Kellermeyer used to be Liz Coen. She recently moved back to her hometown of Denver, Colorado, where she works for Village Voice Media. She would offer to honor any promises of gifts made in her seventh-grade will, but she is sadly no longer in possession of most of them. Heather can still have her makeup, though.

Sarah Kelly is a writer, musician, social worker, and a liar. She currently lives in Brooklyn, New York, with her boom box AND her synthesizer.

Tracie Masek lives in New York City, but was born and raised in Ohio. She watches *The X-Files* every time it is on. *También, habla español.*

Margaret Mason is the author of *No One Cares What You Had for Lunch: 100 Ideas for Your Blog*. She publishes the shopping blogs Mighty Junior and Mighty Goods, which was one of *Time* magazine's Top 50 Cool Sites of the Year. Her personal site, Mighty Girl, has been awesome since 2000. She lives in San Francisco with her husband and son.

Marc Mazique grew up in New Jersey, but now lives in Seattle, Washington. He's been to space camp, played drums in lots of indie bands you've probably never heard of, and reads far too much.

Aaron McQuade is a New York reporter and news anchor for Sirius Satellite Radio. He sorta wishes he had used a fake name for his contributions to this book.

Joshua Neuman is the publisher of *Heeb* magazine. A graduate of Brown University and the Harvard Divinity School, he has taught undergraduate courses in the Philosophy of Religion at New York University, written for *Slate*, ESPN, and Comedy Central and has appeared on VH1, Food Network, Court TV and National Public Radio. His first book, *The Big Book of Jewish Conspiracies*, was published by St. Martin's Press in 2005. His sincerest apologies to all of the women he sent "For INSERT NAME." Seriously.

Joshua Newman kept his diary as a text file on a Macintosh Classic; however, it was for entirely different reasons that *Forbes* called him "a veritable Doogie Howser." He currently lives in New York with his fiancée, and runs the indie film company Cyan Pictures. In 1996, Joshua was Laura Friedman's date to her senior prom.

Sarah Niersbach is a freelance copy editor and graduate student living in Brooklyn, New York. She still avoids nose pickers whenever possible.

Hollie Pocsai is still an overdramatic female living in Hamilton, Ontario. By day, she is a mild-mannered videotape librarian, and by night, she is the sassy coeditor of Love It a Lot (www.LoveItALot.com).

Davy Rothbart creates *Found* magazine (www.FoundMagazine.com), contributes frequent stories to public radio's *This American Life*, and is the author of the story collection *The Lone Surfer of Montana, Kansas*. His work has been featured in *The New Yorker*, the *New York Times*, and *High Times*. He lives in Ann Arbor, Michigan.

Aubrey Sabala is a writer living in San Francisco who continues to insist that her musings at www.AubreySabala.com are part of a website, NOT a blog.

Audrey Shupp Sahns is a graduate of Widener University and worked in the pharmaceutical-research industry until the birth of her first child in 2003. She currently lives with her husband, daughter, and son in suburban Philadelphia. In her spare time she writes about domestic bliss at www.MommyBlahBlahBlog.blogspot.com.

Kitty Joe Sainte-Marie shares a Greenpoint, Brooklyn, railroad apartment with a one-eyed cat and a Turkish delight, photographing and happily living a life less dramatic than in 1996.

Rita Schepok works as a marketing manager in the music industry. In her spare time she is passionate about wine and snowboarding (thankfully not at the same time). Traci, the author of the note, is a Scientist in the School, environmentalist, and storyteller as well as a sailor and a mother of two (usually at the same time). They once again live a stone's throw from each other. They no longer argue about boys—these days they are more likely to share lawn mowers.

John Sellers is the author of *Perfect from Now On: How Indie Rock Saved My Life*. When not contributing to *GQ* or *The Believer*, he rants on his blog, creatively titled Angry John Sellers. He lives in Brooklyn, New York.

Amy Shapiro was conceived in St. Louis, Missouri, in late 1974. Amy is a baker, a blogger, a reader, and a stalker currently living in Brooklyn, New York. Her turn-ons are fat, funny guys and dirty old men. Her turn-offs are germs and rodents. You can read her blog, Dear Diary at www.SoapyT.blogspot.com.

Kristine Smith is a wife and mom in Kansas City with a personal blog at www.FileGirl.com. She still cooks up fantasy phone calls and longs for volatile relationships.

Ariel Meadow Stallings is the author of *Offbeat Bride: Taffeta-Free Alternatives for Independent Brides*. She lives in Seattle, Washington, where she organizes the Salon of Shame, a Cringe-inspired event that's been selling out small theaters since 2005.

Elizabeth Summers operates a salt-crystal manufacturing company in a rural area of the Czech Republic and is an avid collector of red Pyrex. She is no longer opposed to sunlight.

Brad Walsh is a photographer and musician in New York. He runs a nightlife blog at Junk-Mag.com and really, seriously needs to stop buying new socks every weekend. Ray is the only person from high school that he still talks to.

Jessica Wiseman is a self-employed mother of three and writes online about her life at www.Kerflop.com.

About the Author

Sarah Brown is the host and creator of the Cringe Reading Series in Brooklyn, New York. Her writing has appeared online at *McSweeney's, The Morning News, Gawker,* and her personal website, www.QueSeraSera.org. She's been published previously in *Created in Darkness by Troubled Americans: The Best of* McSweeney's *Humor Category.*

Her current diary sucks just as bad as her teenage one. All this crap about self-improvement—hoooo boy, you just would not believe.